ABOUT THAT GOAL

THE OFFICIAL AUTOBIOGRAPHY OF
SEAMUS DARBY
WITH PJ CUNNINGHAM

Ballpoint Press

Published in 2019 by Ballpoint Press
4 Wyndham Park, Bray,
Co Wicklow, Republic of Ireland.

Telephone: 00353 86 821 7631
Email: ballpointpress1@gmail.com
Web: www.ballpointpress.ie

ISBN 978-1-9160863-1-9

Book design and production by Joe Coyle Media&Design,
joecoyledesign@gmail.com

Front cover photograph: Billy Stickland, Inpho Photography
Inset front cover photograph: Colman Doyle, Sportsfile
Inside photographs: Sportsfile, Inpho
and Seamus Darby's personal collection

Printed and bound by GraphyCems

ABOUT THAT GOAL

*This book is dedicated to the memory of
my mother, Janie, and my father, Christy.*

CONTENTS

PART I

PART II

PART III

TALKING BACK...

You get to know a player's strengths and weaknesses very quickly when you mark him during a football match.

Seamus Darby was always friendly both as a player and a person. He had a way of firstly engaging and then disarming you by the way he'd strike up a chat during a game.

It happened to my cost one day when I was playing fullback on the Clara team and he was full-forward on the home side during a league game in Rhode.

"Tell me PJ, is such-and-such still playing with ye?"

I took the bait and explained where the particular person was and why he wasn't playing that day. That led to another question: "What's your man like that's over ye this year?"

Then another. 'Slowly, slowly catchy monkey' as they say.

Near the end of the first half, I was in mid-sentence answering his latest query when he was gone like a shot out of a gun. He stuck the ball past the goalkeeper while I was stuck to the ground like a giant mushroom.

Almost nonchalantly he sidles up to me again and says: "Sorry I missed that last part."

I learned a lesson that day — don't talk to Seamus Darby when you're on duty. More recently though we've talked a lot — and this time around it has been in the line of another type of duty — his book.

It is a privilege to help him write an account of something that is not just sporting, but also cultural and historical in its significance. His is a JFK-like shooting in Dallas moment — 'Where were you when Seamus Darby scored that goal?'

Since that score, thousands of people have told him exactly where they were at the precise moment on September 19, 1982 when the ball flew into the Kerry net. In turn, Seamus is now lifting the lid on his own life and times around and about that goal to set the record straight on issues that have followed him around almost since the final whistle on that date.

PJ Cunningham
August, 2019

HOW THE TEAMS LINED OUT

OFFALY

Martin Furlong

Mick Lowry   Liam O'Connor   Mick Fitzgerald

Pat Fitzgerald   Seán Lowry   Liam Currams

Tomás O'Connor   Padge Dunne

John Guinan   Richie Connor (c)   Gerry Carroll

Johnny Mooney   Matt Connor   Brendan Lowry

Subs: Stephen Darby for M Lowry (24);
Seamus Darby for Guinan (63).
Scorers: M Connor (0-7, 0-6f);
Seamus Darby (1-0); B Lowry (0-3); J Mooney (0-2);
L Currams, P. Fitzgerald and S Lowry (0-1 each).

KERRY

Charlie Nelligan

Ger O'Keeffe   John O'Keeffe   Paudie Lynch

Paídí Ó Sé   Tim Kennelly   Tommy Doyle

Jack O'Shea   SeánieWalsh

Ger Power   Tom Spillane   Ogie Moran

Mikey Sheehy   Eoin Liston   John Egan (c)

Subs: P Spillane for Moran (ht).
Scorers: J Egan (0-3); T. Spillane (0-3); M Sheehy (0-3f);
P Ó Sé, E Liston and S Walsh (0-2 each);
J O'Shea and P Spillane (0-1 each).

FINAL SCORE: OFFALY 1-15 KERRY 0-17

PART I

'DARBY, YOU'LL NEVER KNOW A POOR DAY'

The man said I'd never see a poor day. I don't know who he was but he was so deliriously happy he had to be from Offaly. A short time earlier at the other end of the pitch, I had scored the goal late in the game against Kerry. He was rejoicing like all the other Offaly fans who had just swarmed onto the Croke Park sod.

After GAA President Paddy Buggy presented the cup to Richie Connor, I had tried to make my way to the dressing room. There were people all around me shouting and clapping me on the back. Those time frames passed in slow motion; sound was muffled against the backdrop of hysteria and euphoria. From nowhere, this person caught me in a bear-like embrace and roared into my ear: "Darby, you'll never know a poor day after that."

He gave me a big hug before being swallowed up by the hundreds of other fans also heading for the Offaly dressing room.

The encounter lasted no more than a few fleeting seconds.

He was there.

He was gone.

I never saw him again.

I often wonder who he was or why he would utter such a statement?

All around, the excitement was such that people were pulling and dragging me this way and that. I was on a high with the excitement of it all myself. In the 20 minutes or so since the final whistle, the enormity of what had happened was beginning to sink in.

Scoring the winning goal.

Beating Kerry.

Beating Kerry going for their five-in-a-row.

◆ ◆ ◆ ◆

I was on the pitch the last time Offaly had beaten Kerry in an All-Ireland final in 1972 and while it was a great feeling to beat their team with Mick O'Connell in it, there was no comparison between the occasions.

Back then I was 21, had been around — though not involved playing — the previous breakthrough year against Galway and like most youths, took what was happening in my stride. We won the '72 replay well by 1-19 to 0-13 against Kerry so the result was a foregone conclusion long before the end.

This rainy late Sunday afternoon was different; people were intoxicated with excitement because the game had been so dramatic right up to PJ McGrath's last blow on his whistle.

It was like a wave as people poured onto the playing surface in Croke Park and engulfed each and every Offaly player. Aside from shaking hands with the few Kerry players I met, I was being buffeted this way and that by the force of the swell the crowd was creating. It was all good fun though. It was great. You don't get too many chances to experience something like that in a lifetime.

◆ ◆ ◆ ◆

I don't know for sure how many times since I've had occasion to speak to that stranger who whispered in my ear that wet Sunday — September 19, 1982.

If he'd seen me with nothing in London, depending on the generosity of strangers, sleeping in my clothes and escaping two barrels of a gun through good luck rather than good management, I wonder would he be inclined to say I'd never see a poor day.

It was such a dramatic thing to say when of course he couldn't have known, no more than myself, what the future held.

No one knows how their future will turn out in business, health or relationship issues and I can speak with authority on all of those headings.

Life gives you glimpses of good times but mixes it with plenty of trying times too.

You have to be able to deal with what is thrown at you. And hope that just when you sense life is about to ditch you, something incredible happens and gives you hope again.

Like the Saturday in London just over a decade after I'd scored that goal when I walked out of a pub after 'nursing' a seven-up for two hours while watching the Ireland rugby team being thrashed by England on television.

The man who was supposed to give me a job and a place to sleep had changed his mind. Without paying me for the one shift I'd done the night before, I was penniless. Pride prevented me asking him for the money he owed me because he probably would have said I had got a free bed and we were evens.

It was a chilling moment as I headed out onto Hackney High Street that Saturday afternoon wondering what I would do or where I would go next.

I had no money to get to a house the far side of London where I'd arranged a bed for the night. If I couldn't get there, I would have to consider the prospect of sleeping rough on the city streets.

I had an outside chance of getting to Eddie Ryan who was a friend of a friend. Generously, he had sent word that I could bed down in his place for a few nights if I had no place to stay.

As I approached the lady in the ticket sales booth in the London Underground, my palms were sweaty and my heart was pounding.

"Yes, where are you going to?" she asked, looking me in the eye.

For a moment, I didn't know what to say. Luckily, there was no queue behind me. I then told her: "I want to go to Highbury but I don't have any cash. I do have an Irish chequebook but haven't got a banker's card with me. Would you cash a cheque for a fiver for me?" I asked, trying to remain composed.

She eyed me up and down and I knew the odds were stacked against me. She was about to speak, then stopped, looked into my face again and something changed in her demeanour. She pressed a button and a ticket popped up. Then scanning my eyes again she told me who to make the cheque payable to. I could hardly write with the welling up of emotion — this woman, a complete stranger had thrown me a lifeline at my darkest moment. I've thanked her often down the years for her remarkable courage and thoughtfulness to me that day.

I've found that to be part of my life story — that with ups come the downs, but the most memorable part of it all has been the sheer generosity of nature people have shown me when I'm down and close to out.

CHAPTER 1

A DESTINY OF SORTS

Over the years I've been asked thousands of questions surrounding the goal against Kerry in 1982. Was I going for a goal? Did I push Tommy? Had I ever scored with my left before? Those and many like them I can answer very quickly because it is either a yes or no answer.

Now and then someone will surprise me with a question and I have to deliberate over the answer a bit more. The one that stumped me more than most was when I was asked if I thought it was my destiny to score a goal that will probably live forever in the annals of the GAA because it deprived Kerry of history.

As a young lad more interested in football than books, I never got to hear of Shakespeare's quote about those having greatness thrust upon them. Anyone who knows me will vouch for the fact that I know I was fortunate to score this important goal. I can honestly say that I have no high-falutin airs about what happened other than it did.

I hadn't been much more than an A. N. Other in the '71-'72 winning era and had no desire to be anything other than I was — a bit player behind the stars of that time. I was at best a lieutenant to the generals like Tony McTague, Willie Bryan, Eugene Mulligan and, of course, Paddy McCormack.

I was happy to play that role, yet, there was also something deep down inside me, even after I had been dropped from the panel in '77, which said I would contribute something more to the Offaly cause before I gave up playing altogether.

It was at best a vague — a very vague — awareness that I might have a sort of future history still to come out. All youngsters dream of scoring a goal in the All-Ireland final and I was no different. This, though, was something beyond a boyhood fantasy, something which persisted in the echo of my thoughts that if I ever did get the chance to seize a great moment, I would indeed embrace it.

Mind you, there was a full decade between the two All-Ireland finals in 1972 and 1982. In that 10 year period, there were times when I felt I was totally deranged to even entertain such notions.

The feeling that the door might open on an even bigger day was first spawned in the '72 victory. I clearly remember looking at the stars then — and these lads were like Hollywood idols to me — and thinking that if something similar ever came down the line for me, I would fully relish it. Enjoy every moment of such a high. And you know, that is exactly what I did.

Even in the bad times between being on and then off the county panel, that inner feeling persisted that I hadn't written my last sentence with Offaly. The feeling was enough to keep me half-believing that maybe, maybe somewhere along the line, I'd get my chance.

When the lads reached the All-Ireland Final in 1981 and no one came looking for me through that championship season, it seemed like my race was run. Similarly, the year before I had harboured hopes of a recall but Offaly won the 1980 Leinster title without a need to seek any contribution from me.

The writing was on the wall I felt because the hand of time was turning so that by 1982, I had refused to allow myself to entertain such thoughts.

By then you see, Matt Connor had come on the scene and was the nation's leading scorer. So too had Johnny Mooney, Brendy Lowry, John Guinan, Gerry Carroll and Seánie Lowry had turned himself into an All-Star forward.

In addition, there were other good lads around who were close enough to the panel or had been on it and might be called back in again — the likes of Gerry Hickey, Pat Doyle, Aidan O'Halloran, Tom Fitzpatrick, Vinny Henry, Sean Lawlor, John

Moran and Liam O'Mahony. You could easily count up to a dozen and unlike me, none of them were on the wrong side of 30.

The realist in me said I should be setting my sights more with Rhode in the Offaly club championship rather than Offaly in the Leinster and All-Ireland series. The club became an even greater focus when I was appointed senior team captain in the spring of '82.

Setting out that year, that became my overriding ambition — to lead Rhode to a county title, something that had escaped me over the years.

I wanted to put down a marker with the younger lads in the club by training with renewed vigour during that entire spring. In the league matches, I'd showed up well, winning a lot of ball and kicking a fair few scores too.

I was totally enjoying my football without contemplating any fairytale comebacks onto the county scene. When one of the county selectors, Paddy Fenlon, came into my shop one evening, I thought it was for the usual chat on all things GAA. Initially that was the case but then he truly shocked me by confidentially telling me that Eugene McGee and all the selectors would be at the upcoming championship match against Daingean with the intention of bringing me back into the Offaly squad.

Immediately, that turned the optimistic bulb on inside my head again. It was like a prophesy had been part fulfilled and now I decided that I would give everything 100 per cent to make that long held inner feeling come true.

I'd attended the All-Ireland final in 1981 with the rest of the seventies winning Offaly teams who were by then mostly retired. I saw at first hand how McGee had brought the group a step further every year since he took charge from the '77 championship. I reckoned that on the law of averages Offaly had a great chance of winning the All-Ireland in '82 — and now I had the opportunity to be part of it.

Getting back on the panel and giving myself the chance to see what that destiny might be drove me on. I couldn't get enough training and I couldn't get enough football. I was like a kid being given a new toy.

I lost a stone in less than a month and was picked for and played well in the Leinster final against Dublin, scoring 1-3. Just as I was about to embrace the dream again, my hamstring went in that game and I missed the All-Ireland semi-final against Galway.

Johnny Mooney came in for me in that game and played so well that I knew there was no chance I would be starting in the final against Kerry. I knew the best I could hope for would be to come in as a sub and hopefully do something memorable.

In truth, I thought I'd be introduced much earlier in that game. It had got so late that I'd almost given up hope of getting a run at all. Then McGee shouted:

"Seamus Darby, get ready."

At last I had got the call.

As it transpired, I did have a date with destiny and I didn't have long to wait for it to be fulfilled.

As in life, sometimes your sporting dreams do come true too.

CHAPTER 2

IS THERE A GOAL IN THE GAME?

I had my own thinking done before I went on the field to tell you the truth. Looking out at the game, I felt that whoever scored a goal was going to win — if Kerry got it we were gone and if we got it, we might snatch it at the death.

Eugene (McGee) had told me there wasn't time to win the game unless we got a goal, which is why he wanted me to stay in close. Going onto the pitch, I said to myself: "If I get a kick of this ball, I'm going for goal — that's for certain."

I didn't get the first ball into my hands because in the mad scramble, the ball was like a hot potato and although I almost had it at one stage, it was knocked out of my grasp. I nearly fell over as it was worked away from me by the Kerry players. It was cleared up the field from the patch where I finally would get my only possession in the game a few minutes later.

Anyone who has ever played for a team knows that if you go on as a sub, it does wonders for your confidence if you manage to get possession fairly quickly.

I hadn't been able to do that and it annoyed me but I also knew that the last thing Offaly needed me to do was to follow the ball out in the hope of getting a touch. I resisted that temptation though I knew it was quite possible that another ball might not come my way by the time the final whistle sounded.

So I banished such negative thoughts. I knew Offaly needed a goal and to score it, I also knew that I needed to remain in close. Striking distance. Matt was also thinking along those lines because he had positioned himself about the same distance from goal as me, except he was over on the right. By chipping away at the Kerry lead with points from frees, he had set up the possibility of a goal winning the game for us. My experience told me to be patient...to hold my nerve and provide an option to the lads out the field should they want to get the ball in.

As I recall the build up to the goal, there is a reel in my head that starts to spin with 'Bomber' fouling Pat Fitzgerald. Seánie Lowry takes the ball, casually places it on the ground and moves upfield as if he is on a Sunday stroll after his lunch. I see Pat Fitzgerald trying to compose himself from the tackle as the responsibility of taking the kick rests with him. He jabs the ball forward to Richie Connor about 25 yards away. Richie collects and hand passes it to his first cousin, Liam, who has forsaken his defensive duties to burst forward as an added attacking option. He hops the ball between those giant strides of his and is around the Kerry 45 metre line when Seán Walsh tries to close him down. He's just a yard too far away to make contact. Liam releases a perfectly flighted ball in a cross-field arc. I see it is coming in my general direction down at the Railway end.

At that stage I didn't know if I would get possession, never mind decide which foot I would use to take a shot. I had a preference for my right, particularly if I won the ball directly in front of the goal. Equally, it never cost me a thought to turn onto my left as I was comfortable shooting off that side as well.

In this instance, my mind was made up for me to some extent as I could see a couple of Kerry players — Jacko (O'Shea) and Johnno (O'Keeffe) — were circling to block off the middle in front of the goal. That persuaded me to turn away from the possibility of being blocked.

With the ball in flight, the biggest problem in my head was — would I be able to get it into my hands? I wasn't quite sure of my bearings — part of me thought I might be 25 yards out while another part was worried that I was just in front of Charlie Nelligan. I had a fear that he could get a run and jump higher than Tommy or me to clear the ball with his fist.

As I landed with the ball, I discovered that I was actually straddling the 13-metre line. The rest was pure instinct. I pulled the ball down to my right side both to protect it and to prepare for a left-footed shot. I didn't have to think that — it worked itself out. Almost in the same motion, I swung with my left boot after seeing that Charlie had stayed on his line. Moments later, he was spread-eagled on the ground after just failing to make contact with the flight of the ball.

My aim was to get the ball over Charlie and under the bar. As it happened — and this is where luck plays its part — I hit it right on the button. Charlie said afterwards that he felt the wind of the ball going past his hands... he was a fingernail or two away from getting it and possibly making the save of the century.

What a time to strike a perfect shot...and with my left foot. It was like hitting the ideal golf shot, the ping was sublime. It was so on the money that I didn't even feel the contact.

Yet for a mega-second, I had a doubt over whether the ball had gone into the net at all. I suspended belief until I saw the umpire bend to pick up the green flag.

I knew then it was a goal alright.

I go into a bubble at this juncture; I'm aware I'm celebrating but for a second everything goes quiet. It was like the volume has been turned right down around Croke Park.

I'm jumping up and down in sheer ecstasy. Even then, a part of me is wondering — "Is this really happening or am I dreaming?"

The noise suddenly returns like someone has turned a switch on. And what an unreal sound it is. It's a noise I've never heard before. Brendy (Lowry) is with me celebrating when the thought hits me like a sledgehammer: "Where's the kick out going?"

I shout at him: "Brendy, for f**k sake will you get a man, this is Kerry we're playing."

As it turned out that was the only possession I got in the game. For the final few minutes, I am basically a spectator, with the perfect vantage point to see the action further down the pitch. I'm only able to process little snippets of what's happening on the field of play. It's hard to concentrate. The ball bubbles around with both sides in possession.

Johnny Mooney gets it under the Hogan Stand. I'm happy because I know he never loses a ball... Gerry Carroll has the chance to score but his effort drifts wide... and then sometime later, he loses possession on the other side and the ball is picked up by Páidí who kicks the ball long and high into our territory.

Are we going to give away an equaliser? The thought is too heavy to hold. I shout down the field hoping lads a hundred yards away can hear. "Tackle. Lads, tackle. Don't foul. For f**k sake, no frees."

The ball is played in and Tom Spillane is fastening onto it. I've gone now from the fear of a point being scored to force a draw to a new realisation — that a goal will win it for Kerry. Out of nowhere Stephen appears and almost unseen, he jabs the ball out of Spillane's possession. Good man Stephen!

The reel runs on. When I focus again, the ball has spilled but somehow Martin Furlong has it. It's a perilous hold on possession and he knows that. He's brought the ball across the end line; he wants to get it out of the danger area.

It's manic but no better man than Furlong to do the right thing.

We're trying to get out and Kerry are fighting with all their might for that one last chance. Mikey Sheehy intercepts a pass but the angle is so acute, he steers the ball across the goal in the hope a colleague will win possession.

Instead, Seánie's at home in Furlong's absence; he's the man in the right place at the right time. How often has that been the case? He catches the ball the far side of the 'square,' dummies an opponent and is heading out towards the 13-metre line when I see him lift the ball triumphantly over his head — he has heard the final whistle before me and is celebrating as he continues his run forward.

When the final whistle sounded, I'm still standing more or less in the same place where I had scored the goal. Tommy is beside me. We shake hands and before I can do or say anything, the crowd is swarming on the pitch.

Things are running through my mind in black and white flashbacks of my boyhood days. I see my parents in the house at home and I'm imagining the fellas I played with as a young lad in those 'All-Irelands' we played every Sunday behind Ballybryan National School. The reel jumps into the present time and I'm wondering how my wife, Veronne, is coping as she is days away from delivering our third baby. Then I catch a glimpse of my brother, Stephen in the distant haze and he too is shaking hands with the man he marked, the Kerry captain, John Egan.

I want to get down to him, to hug him and celebrate such a day of glory as brothers. To thank him for the part he played in making sure I had scored what proved to be the winning goal in an All-Ireland final.

I want to get down to him but I know it's impossible — there's a surge of supporters tossing me every which way but where I want to go. It's the madness of winning an All-Ireland and I'm more than happy to go with the flow.

I have long accepted that this goal no longer belongs to me or my teammates or even Offaly people in general. It belongs to Irish people all over the world who love our national games and take pride in following them.

CHAPTER 3

ABOUT THAT GOAL

There is one thing that baffles me about that goal — how it appears to still have so much relevance this far down the road from September, 1982.

I knew once we had won and stopped Kerry achieving an historic five-in-a-row it would thrust me into the spotlight for a while — and it certainly did that.

I just didn't get how totally different it would be. Yes, there was the Kerry factor, stopping history being made and all that. And, yes, there was the heightened drama of a late goal.

I knew that Martin Furlong and myself would be the central figures of the coverage because of what had happened in the game. He got the Man of the Match for his penalty save and would later get the Player of the Year award. And rightly so.

Obviously though, a goalscorer attracts the headlines and the cameras and microphones were everywhere I went. The following week I did countless interviews on RTE radio and television, which was the only real broadcasting presence in Ireland at the time.

When our third child arrived a few weeks later, we were on the front page of that weekend's Sunday Independent. Apparently, the goal resonated beyond sport into people's lives...but in my wildest dreams, I never saw it going on forever.

I thought the invites to functions would be a flavour of the month thing which would have finite relevance as time went by. I was pretty sure it would all dry up after six months or certainly before the following year's All-Ireland. When Dublin dethroned us in '83 in the Leinster Final and went on to win the Sam Maguire cup with 12 players in a much different type of never-to-be-forgotten final against Galway, I felt sure I would be handing over the baton.

But the invites kept coming. I thought to myself that logically there must come a time when I would fade into the background as more All-Irelands were being played, and won and lost, creating their own heroes, their own stories.

But year in, year out from then — and we are talking 37 years now as this is being written — I am still asked to go to places in the four corners of the country to present medals, to open GAA events, to participate in Q&As and to help fundraise for good causes.

The endurance of that one sporting moment in time is something I honestly can't understand.

I was 31 when I scored it — I'm now 68 and after the experience of the intervening years, I can envisage being asked to attend events till my toes are tied together.

I have long accepted that this goal no longer belongs to me or my teammates or even Offaly people in general. It belongs to Irish people all over the world who love our national games and take pride in following them.

I've lost count of the number of people who have come up to me, many with tears in their eyes, to tell me where they were at the game or at home when the ball hit the back of the net. It is a 'where were you moment?' and it survives and even thrives because of the context and drama that surrounds it.

Kerry were on the cusp of history and that made the game special in itself. Then Mícheál O'Hehir, the RTE commentator, added to the suspense as the minutes ticked away by hinting more than once that there might be big drama ahead.

It was years after playing in the game that I listened to his commentary and there is no doubt that he had a sixth sense operating that day.

When he asked if there was a goal in the game, it was as if he was visualising what was about to happen — the tension increased because he didn't say if it was Kerry or Offaly who might score it. He brought the notion of a fairytale ending to the forefront of every viewer's mind — and left it hanging there.

I remember big sporting occasions when I was growing up — Fionavon winning the Grand National, Down becoming the first team to bring Sam Maguire across the border and Cassius Clay (Muhammad Ali) doing what all the old people thought was impossible — beating Sonny Liston.

For Irish people, that goal is one of those 'where were you moments?' and I'm humbled that I got the opportunity to score it.

◆ ◆ ◆ ◆

It is not the same for Kerry folk and I was intrigued watching the documentary on Mick O'Dwyer broadcast within the last year where he claimed that the goal still haunts him.

I only found out recently too how Tommy Doyle had to endure so much poison from within his own county boundaries (see next chapter). I know from having become friendly with a number of Kerry players of the time that it is something that never quite goes away, despite the staggering achievements of O'Dwyer leading them from a four-in-a-row ('78-'81) to a three-in-a-row ('84-'86).

The documentary entitled 'Micko' shown on RTÉ had a line from the old maestro which said the goal was "implanted in my mind."

I thought it was a great way to describe its effect — for some reason even at this remove, it manages to be 'implanted' in the GAA public consciousness.

You can't but love Micko and I knew as soon as the goal was mentioned, he'd get in a mention about "the push". And sure enough he obliged.

He told the camera: "A little nudge made history. If you were well beaten, you'd be happy enough. I mean, we were so close. I was sick. It's like a death in the family, if that's possible.

I think of it at least once a week. It would still be implanted in my mind."

◆ ◆ ◆ ◆

Not a day goes by but someone mentions the goal. Often it is a stranger but sometimes it is also used by my so-called pals from the panel to keep me in my place.

The Lowrys are great people to slag and in my case, Seánie usually takes the lead. He teased me about it one day when we were playing golf out in Esker Hills... "Darby, how does a one-kick-wonder of a sub only on for seven minutes grab all the headlines for Offaly's win?"

You have to give as good as you get with these jokers so I do. I answered back: –"Seánie, can you imagine what I'd have done if I was on for the full 70 minutes?"

He repeated our conversation on one of the documentaries but in fairness to him, he also included my retort, adding: "I suppose he had a point."

For all of the things that brought me joy from scoring that goal, the one negative feeling I carry is that it didn't get goal of the year in 1982. I was very disappointed and what was worse, it didn't even finish as runner up. Seán Ó Síocháin, the Ard Stiúrthoir of the GAA at that time, was the adjudicator and he put the goal by Kerry's Mikey Sheehy against Cork in the Munster Final replay as the winner.

It was a really good goal the way Mikey came flying through but Kerry were winning well at the time he scored it. The other goal that beat me into third place was scored by John McCormack of Longford from a Leinster championship match against Dublin in Tullamore. I was very unhappy about that decision because genuinely I think it was a poor one. I think time has proven Mr Ó Síocháin might have got that one wrong.

CHAPTER 4
TOMMY DOYLE
AND THE GOAL

About that goal — everyone has a theory on the moments leading up to it. The one I've heard most often from those who think it was a foul is: "Ah, I saw you... you put your hand on his back and pushed him."

If you play back the game on video, you'll see that I didn't put my hands near my marker Tommy Doyle's back for the seven minutes or so I was on as a sub in the 1982 All-Ireland final.

I know exactly what I did — I pressed my upper left arm into the side of his shoulder to gently 'negotiate' Tommy away from the flight of the ball that was rapidly descending between us. Definitely, mine was a 'leaning in' motion. I don't deny that.

Whether you'd define it as 'a nudge,' as Micko called it, 'a push' as others have stated or 'a poke' or 'a prod,' the reality is the referee PJ McGrath didn't blow for a foul.

In my opinion, having watched it back countless times, it would have been hard had he given a free out. That said, there was contact, albeit of a low-level intensity and I'm sure there are people (particularly in Kerry) who feel the whistle could have been blown — and I can accept that view too.

Personally, I think the legendary Kerry full-back, Joe Keohane, who was a selector with Micko, got it spot on when he said: "What Darby did was within the legitimate range of pushing without transcending into being a foul."

My mindset in that moment was that I had to get the ball because I felt pretty sure there wouldn't be another chance. The way Liam kicked the ball from the right side of the pitch across to the left side of goal favoured Tommy slightly as he was out in front of me. My concern was that he was going to catch the ball, burst out and clear it upfield. If that had happened, I would have been in trouble with the Offaly crowd and there would not have been much talk afterwards about Seamus Darby.

I had to use my body to ease him over a little to improve my chances. That's what I did and it sent him slightly forward.

It was the instinct that came from learning your trade being a small man in Offaly club football. You discover ways to ensure that the ball falls into your hands instead of your opponents. I was only putting my long apprenticeship into practice.

Tommy and I got to know each other well down the years after the two of us became the centre of attention for different reasons after that match. For as sure as I was given the star-ring role of hero, he was cast, particularly by Kerry fans, as the villain of the piece.

His critics said he was naïve to allow me catch the ball and that somehow it was all his fault that Kerry didn't win the five-in-a-row.

I often thought of Tommy in the weeks and months after the game and hoped he was coping with the abuse that I sensed would be hurled in his direction.

There may also have been guilt on my part because there was contact between us and he could easily have come out and said in his own defence that it was a push and therefore a foul. He would have been entitled to do that. To his credit he never did; instead he took the haymaker on the chin and I admired him greatly for showing such character in adversity.

The wheel of fortune goes around as we all know and I don't suppose there were too many outside Kerry happier than myself in 1986 when Tommy not only won another — his seventh — All-Ireland medal, but captained the Kingdom to glory as well.

As I watched him lift the Sam Maguire over his head in Croke Park that day, I felt a huge surge of pride and satisfaction inside. I suppose it is like the sort of feeling you experience if a member of your family achieves something.

I was close to tears. I knew from that moment that Tommy could walk down the streets of Tralee, Killarney or any other town or village in Kerry — and look people in the eye who had been calling him every sort of name following the '82 final.

Yes, he had won six All-Irelands before the 1986 final against Tyrone but this one — when he was captain — seemed more like redemption.

There had been no five-in-a-row but Kerry under Micko had backed up their four-in-a-row with this — a three-in-a-row. At least that was the way I looked on it from the outside– and I was absolutely thrilled to see a good, decent guy, as Tommy certainly is, end up as the main man.

Tommy also won three All Stars in a row in '84, '85 and '86 — the years after the 'push' incident. That also showed the true mettle of the man. He drove the toxic tongues down the throats of his detractors with the consistent high level of performance he achieved after '82.

Around the time of the 1986 All-Ireland, I was working as a rep driving all over Ireland. I knew I would be in his neck of the woods over the following fortnight and I wanted to meet up with him. Tommy was also a rep — he was with a beer company while I was selling wallpaper across the 26 counties.

We hadn't arranged a rendezvous before I set out and in a time when there was no internet or mobile phones, making contact was much harder. I was in Kerry getting orders and supplying wallpaper and I wanted to get my work done before I went looking for him.

I was walking down the street when I just happened to bump into him in the middle of Killarney. If I had planned it, it couldn't have worked out any better. Naturally, we went for one. That turned into another and in the end we spent most of the night out together.

What did we talk about? Well, I know I told him how happy I was that he was captain and had led Kerry to an incredible achievement on top of what they had achieved before the '82 final. And he was a hero now in Kerry eyes and feck any begrudgers who were left.

Tommy and I would talk about everything except the goal. Neither of us ever brought it up directly. We probably knew what each other thought — and simply left it at that.

I think it was the time together in Killarney that cemented our friendship. We had a long chat that evening and it created a bond. It was one of the good things for both of us that came out of that goal.

In the aftermath of the 1982 game, I know I was thinking purely about the goal from my own and Offaly's perspective. There was so much backslapping with people around me celebrating our victory that Sunday night that I had little or no time to think of Tommy. That's the truth.

I was shocked the day after when Mikey Sheehy and Jacko met me at the lunch for both teams at the Burlington Hotel, which was the tradition at the time.

I'd looked around to see if I could see Tommy but he wasn't there. I asked the lads where he was and they said he was feeling pretty low after what happened and had decided to skip the event. They suggested that maybe I should give him a ring.

Now I was really upset; both with myself for not thinking that for every upside, someone has a downside and also because I now knew for sure that Tommy was suffering.

The last thing I'd ever want to be is in the limelight at someone else's expense. Sport does that, it turns out heroes and villains and when you are on the wrong side, it can be a very lonely place to be.

As I had just found out.

I gave Tommy a ring as the lads suggested sometime later

and we talked for a few minutes. I don't know what we said, but I think we agreed to meet up the next time either of us were in Offaly or Kerry.

I can't put a true timeline on it, it might have been the following year, but I remember my Rhode and Offaly teammate Jody Gunning, myself and our two wives and kids were on a break in Kerry and we went into Tommy's pub which he was renting in Tralee at the time.

Tommy gave us the royal treatment on his premises. As always we had a great chat about football and how Kerry and Offaly were looking that year. Not a word about the other. I was thankful for that and I know he was as well. Even Jody, who'd be a good man to hop a ball any time of the day or night, was aware of the sensitivity and instead he (Jody) allowed us to slag him about how poor a referee he was becoming.

We didn't see each other much after that for a good while. Like myself, Tommy had his ups and downs in his enterprises and went to London to try his hand at the business over there. When I was over there myself, I tried to look him up after one of the Kerry lads told me the name of the pub he was managing.

I remember it was a fairly long journey from where I was renting but one day I jumped on the tube, then took a bus and arrived at the premises. I went out to his place on the off chance that he would be there. I think it was called the Bridge House — there was no sign of him behind the bar. I asked the barman if Tommy was around. He told me he had given up the pub a short time before and as far as he knew, he'd gone back to work in Ireland.

I left it at that for a while because like him, I was too busy trying to sort out my life and had precious little time for anything else. I couldn't afford to fly over and back or take time off to go to Kerry; I had to knuckle down and see if I could save a few bob.

Tommy and I have met up many times since and I can tell you he's done me several good turns. I remember there was one time a player I knew in Offaly had applied for a job which Tommy had the power to give out. We chatted about it and when he came back to me, the young lad was delighted to tell me he had got the position.

That goal though is never far away from either of us. I am all too aware that it is liable to crop up at any time in any company. I remember a night shortly after I had bought the 'The Greyhound Bar' in Toomevara when the place was packed. Tipp FM do a live show called 'Down Your Way' which is presented by Eamon O'Dwyer and I was the subject of their attention in this particular programme. I had invited Tommy and his wife up for the occasion and they stayed overnight with us.

There was a great atmosphere and people from all over the midlands as well as Tipperary came in for the special occasion. One of the people there was a regular, a really lovely man called Charlie Murphy, who originally hailed from Ballylongford in Kerry.

As the radio interviewer was talking, Charlie was propped up in his usual place in the corner where he always stood when he was having a drink in our place.

Eamon was interviewing Tommy and me and said something about the 'push.' Tommy shrugged it off, saying nothing more than: "The ref didn't blow it," and left it at that.

I followed by saying something similar: "Some refs would blow for a foul and others would let it go." That sort of thing.

We were trying to tiptoe around the issue which, of course, is the real question journalists always want to have answered.

Just as the Tipp FM man was about to move on to next topic, Charlie shouted as clear as day from the background: "He did f**king push you, Tommy."

That went out live across the airwaves and everyone laughed — except the horrified presenter. I knew then that one of my customers, Lord have mercy on him, went to his grave convinced that I had committed a foul before scoring the goal.

I'd do anything for Tommy and he has always been the

same for me. Over the years, a few of us in Offaly have got very close to a group from that Kerry team. We've stayed in touch and became very friendly with the likes of Seánie Walsh, the Bomber, Mikey Sheehy, Ógie Moran and we knew Páidí, God rest him, very well too.

They're all sound fellas — not saying the others I haven't mentioned aren't — but these lads like to play a bit of golf and have a bit of craic afterwards. So we enjoy meeting up.

◆ ◆ ◆ ◆

It was late last year when I became aware for the first time of the level of abuse that Tommy had to endure over my goal.

Someone I know heard an interview with him on Radio Kerry last August and recorded it for me. I think the show went out shortly after the terrible criticism Eamon Fitzmaurice had to put up with when Kerry were knocked out of the inaugural Super 8 series when they didn't qualify for the All-Ireland semi-finals.

As everyone knows, Tommy is not one who likes the sound of his own voice or sets out to make headlines. On this occasion, he came out forcefully about the misuse of social media and the harm it was doing in the GAA.

During the interview, he spoke for the first time publicly about the sack-loads of hate mail he got in the post, berating him for Kerry's failure to win the five-in-a-row. Up to then, he only ever confided in a few people very close to him about what had happened.

Tommy explained that he didn't have long to wait for the critics to come at him — he got it once the final whistle was blown in Croke Park.

"I had hardly finished shaking hands with Seamus Darby beside me when I got hit by a left hook," he revealed.

He said he was in a state of shock, like the rest of the team, after the match ended but he was knocked down to the ground by that box from a so-called Kerry supporter, with four or five other fellas shouting at him: "You cost us ten thousand pounds."

A number of Kerry Co Board officials saw what happened and immediately came to his aid as the cowards ran off into the crowd.

Referring to what Eamonn Fitzmaurice was getting in the neck after Kerry interest in the 2018 championship ended, Tommy went on: "The GAA is a great organisation, but this isn't what it's all about. I'd like these people to understand that I came through quite a lot of it myself.

"You remember the letters — of course you will, but the older you get, the less you take it to heart. I never mentioned much about them because in our time you would be a bit embarrassed about it. I was lucky to have the likes of Micko and Páidí to see me through it.

"The Kerry team is our prized possession and it's the same in every other county. I want to see young people play GAA and not be turned off it. I'd hate to think that people wouldn't want their kids to play for Kerry. You have to go through a lot. This type of thing's getting too much publicity and is not helping the GAA," he stated.

Tommy told the programme he felt Fitzmaurice had done a fantastic job for Kerry and the poison being put out on social media was totally out of order.

He said he himself had got some real "bad letters, really nasty stuff" which was exacerbated because they lost out again in '83, that time to Cork in the Munster Final.

"I got anonymous letters then, but social media brings it to another level entirely," he said. He mentioned how Micheál Donoghue, the Galway hurling manager, in the same fashion as Eamonn, had been shot down on Twitter and Facebook and the like. "To be truthful, initially I wasn't going to say anything about it but when I saw people raising it, I said I'd say it's not on anymore."

◆ ◆ ◆ ◆

Tommy and I arranged that he'd call in to me for breakfast on his way to Eugene McGee's funeral last May. We were both very sad at the passing but had a good chat about different things that morning. It would have been lovely for the two of us to drive up to Longford together but he had to be back for a certain time and I knew I'd be there with the Offaly boys until very late.

We met up again that day at the church and three of us sat together in the same pew — Tommy and the two guys he marked in the final, John Guinan and myself.

After the ceremony we were hanging around outside the church, and Guinan winked at me behind Tommy's back and says: "C'mon Darby, we have him now."

The three of us laughed. One time sporting adversaries who are bound together by the great legacies of 1982 — it gave both sides new friends for life.

The late Weeshie Fogarty probably summed the whole 1982 episode up better than anyone when he wrote an article commemorating the 25th anniversary of the occasion.

"What occurred at the Railway End goal in Croke Park 25 years ago is the most talked about incident in the history of Gaelic games and the name Seamus Darby will be forever associated with Kerry football."

As an Offalyman I like that line of being associated with Kerry football. It's an honour and I cherish it.

*Wouldn't it have been nice
if the three of us had arranged
to sit down for half an hour
and share the memory of our
perspective on that goal?*

CHAPTER 5

GOOD ENOUGH FOR ME AND EUGENE McGEE

It's at times like this that you have little regrets that you never got round to saying things. It's the evening of May 9 this year and I'm driving home from the graveyard in Aughnacliffe in Co Longford after Eugene McGee's funeral. Inevitably, I'm thinking back to the time he brought me back into the panel in June '82 and also to the day of the final on September 19, of that same year.

We probably had met hundreds of times since that day and we never sat down to talk about its impact on both of us. I mean Eugene and myself are defined in some measure by the outcome of that game and just as I had the same thoughts coming back from Liam O'Connor's funeral in Waterford five years before that, there is a sadness that we never got to talk through what had happened.

It was Eugene who decided that a 31-year-old could still play a role in his own ambition to become an All-Ireland winning manager. It was Liam, who not only did a marvellous job curbing the effectiveness of the great 'Bomber' but strayed up field to deliver the final pass, and it was Seamus Darby, yours truly, who got the opportunity to score that goal.

Wouldn't it have been nice if the three of us had arranged to sit down for half an hour and share the memory of our perspective on that goal?

As I'm driving back through the midlands this evening, I start to dwell on the McGee and O'Connor families and their losses. I think how Marian is the one who has suffered most with the loss of her brother and husband from our Offaly fold.

My own little regrets are insignificant compared to how the family are feeling but it doesn't stop me from wishing I had taken the time to meet and relive the memory of the day.

When Eugene arrived in Offaly as manager in late 1976, the wheels were coming off the squad that had won three Leinsters and back-to-back All-Irelands in the early seventies. Kevin Kilmurray was about the only Offaly player I knew who had gone to university at the time and seemingly he had been very influential in getting Eugene into the county.

He had worked under him at UCD which was the best club team of the seventies, winning Sigerson Cup, Dublin and All-Ireland championships. This mysterious Eugene McGee was at the centre of it but no one knew what he looked like the first night he presented himself at training.

It certainly wasn't the easiest place for a young man to enter and make an instant impression. Fr. Gilhooley had the advantage of being around most of the '71-'72 squad from the time they were minors and the fact that he was a member of the clergy also gave him instant respect in the Ireland of that time.

I wasn't there the first night John Dowling as Co Secretary and Fr. Heaney as Co Chairman introduced him to the panel in late 1976. He was inheriting a dressing-room of very strong characters — some of whom were only a few years younger than himself — and they wouldn't be the kind to take any bullshit.

These guys had their Celtic Crosses and looking back, you can only admire the bravery of Eugene to take charge of a squad that was past its sell-by-date with the enthusiasm that he did.

Shortly before he arrived, I suffered one of the few injuries which prevented me from either training or playing. It happened in a club game between Rhode and Clara. Their big midfielder, Noelie McCarthy, caught a free kick into his own square and as he came down with the ball, his two knees landed on my back as we both fell to the ground.

I remember McGee pulled me aside one night early in his tenure at a time when my club mate, Gerry Hickey, was also injured. He asked me what the story was and I told him I was crippled with back pain. He told me it wouldn't go away by itself and I should get something done quickly about it.

There and then I asked Gerry if he would drive me down to Johnstown to see Ossie Bennett, who was a renowned in Offaly as the best 'rub' man in the business. Gerry agreed.

We didn't get there until half ten but Ossie was still working in his garage when we arrived. He brought me inside to the house, put me lying down on my back on his bench. He lifted my legs up and I heard a click. Ossie then twisted me and I heard another click. Now I don't know what he did or how he did it but from that night I never had a problem with my back while I was playing.

With all the stuff Eugene was dealing with in his early days in Offaly, I wouldn't blame him in the slightest for thinking that Seamus Darby was a lazy little bastard. Between that injury — and sometimes back injuries can be used as an excuse not to train — and then not being in great shape for the early National Football league games, I would even have thought that myself. It would be years later before he found out I was one of the better trainers once I was involved with his '82 squad when it was at the right time of year.

I saw very little of Eugene during his first five years in Offaly; I wasn't close to him and in all honesty there probably wasn't too many who were.

For a man who didn't kick football himself, I have to give him an awful lot of credit for how he dealt with the situations he found himself in, particularly those early times. He went about his work with a great degree of intelligence and from early on, you could see he wasn't fearful of reputations and was single-minded enough to do what needed to be done.

When you think about it, he had a good apprenticeship in handling big names — Kerry's John O'Keeffe and Jackie Walsh,

Wexford's Mick Carty, Garrett O'Reilly from Cavan, Colm O'Rourke and Gerry McEntee from Meath all were involved at some stage with him in UCD.

Eugene got rid of some of the older lads who no longer had the legs for inter-county football... he kept on the likes of Willie Bryan, Eugene Mulligan, Paddy Fenning, Mick Wright, Kilmurray and a few others who would serve him well in transitioning the side back into provincial winners.

He rooted out anyone he thought wasn't going to add to his panel. This was the right thing to do even if we didn't think so at the time.

He dropped Martin Furlong because he didn't kick out the ball. Other 'keepers in the country had the same problem as Furlong because the tradition at county level was for a full-back like Paddy McCormack or a corner back like Donie O'Sullivan in Kerry to take all the kick outs.

Imagine if Furlong had taken the hump and never gone back. Imagine if he hadn't been ambitious enough to practise getting length into his kick-outs. Imagine if McGee hadn't the sense to see that Furlong brought more than just an ordinary goalkeeper's value to a team.

It's incredible to think that his kick outs became good enough to help Offaly mount their charge in the late seventies and early eighties for All-Ireland glory. Martin collected three successive All-Stars for the goalkeeping position as well as being named GAA footballer of the year in '82.

People will tell you that one of Eugene's great traits from the day he arrived was that he listened. So when those he trusted told him how special Furlong was, he got him back in after the goalkeeping horror show from his first year (1977) in charge against Wexford in the Leinster championship at Croke Park and never had a problem again until '84. That was a time when Furlong was suffering from rheumatoid arthritis that badly restricted movement in his arms. Laz Molloy had to be summoned from the Hogan Stand and he played the second half against Longford in Croke Park when the normal stand-in Dinny Wynne had a bad day at the office.

Side by side with Furlong came Seánie Lowry from that earlier era. Again McGee had the cop on to see what this guy brought to a set-up — and it was way beyond what he contributed as a player. That is not to take away from what Seánie could do on the field — he was our only All-Star in 1979. That came largely on the strength of his 0-10 against Dublin in that disaster of a Leinster Final when we had the title in our hands but let it slip.

Furlong was a stand-in captain to Richie Connor and Seánie had no such title but they were all leaders in that dressing-room. That is the first commandment of creating a winning side — get your leaders in place and they will steer the ship for you.

McGee was a great planner and tactician and a deep thinker around the game — he was well ahead of his time. Back in the seventies, he provided every member of the team and subs with a typewritten dossier of who they were likely to be playing against — also giving info such as your opponents weaknesses and strengths — how a certain player might like to turn to the right or the other way.

I'd never encountered such detail and his ability to say things that emboldened you to try something was understated but real. For instance, as I refer elsewhere in the book, the night he brought me back into the panel in June '82, he introduced me to the panel by saying the reason I was there was because I was currently the best forward in Offaly.

With the calibre of All Star forwards present and listening to him, he had already made me a better player just by uttering those few words. The night of that Offaly call up came 11 years after Fr. Gilhooley decided to include me for the first time in his plans in 1971.

I actually lined out for Edenderry against Rhode one year - 1989 - in the Offaly championship when I was marked by my brother Stephen in the county semi-final.

CHAPTER 6
THE GROWING-UP YEARS

I was born three and a half miles from Rhode in a place called Ballybrittan and if our house had been built on the other side of the road, I would have been in Edenderry parish and played most of my club football in red rather than the green and gold of Rhode.

Stephen, my brother, another former Offaly player Gerry Hickey and myself often wondered what it would have been like if we had played with Edenderry. I actually lined out for them one year — 1989 — in the Offaly championship when I was marked by Stephen in the county semi-final. That story is told elsewhere in this book.

When I was three or four, we moved closer to Rhode and then it was the canal and the road that divided us from the Edenderry parish. I went to school in Ballybryan, the eldest of eight children. On my first day, Noel Hickey was recruited by my mother to bring me there and home on his bike. This was something of a milestone in my mother's life as I was the first of her brood out the door. I can still hear her telling Noel to mind me and look after me in the schoolyard, which to his credit he did very well.

My mother, Janie Gorman, originally hailed from Carbury in Co Kildare. When she met my father Christy, a farm labourer, she was living in Rhode and working in the Edenderry Shoe Factory. When my mother and father got married in 1944, they had to wait a long time for the stork to deliver their first child — me.

They were married seven years before I arrived and then they ended up blessed with another seven. Years later when my father heard one of the Offaly players from the '82 team, Mick Lowry and his wife Margaret had children after many years of waiting, he shared a joke with him. They met going into a football match in O'Connor Park, Tullamore one Sunday. Daddy held out his hand and congratulated Mick on his new arrival.

"About time," responded Mick.

"You were in the same boat as me," explained my father. "I had to send the wife off to Knock to get her started but when she brought home the eighth child to the house, I had to send her to Lourdes to get her to stop," he laughed.

Daddy worked every hour God sent him and as his eldest and able lieutenant at home, I was expected to do the same. We didn't have any land, only a big back garden but we always had a few cows on the canal bank, a few calves to provide for every year as well as a couple of pigs and a flock of hens out the back. The cows grazed the long acre and it was my duty to find them along the canal bank, and milk them morning and night.

Daddy would never have been on big money in his lifetime — small wages were the order of the day in the fifties. However, we had our own eggs, milk, spuds, vegetables and the odd chicken to feed our large family. First communions and confirmations came thick and fast as an extra expense on my parents and that's where selling the pigs or a calf came in handy when my mother had to buy us new clothes for those special occasions.

My first job every morning was to milk the cows and my last task after milking them in the evenings was to feed the calves and pigs. In time, Stephen would row in and help but he was over three and a half years younger than me, so I was out on my own for a good while doing these chores.

We also had additional chores that took up most of our summer holidays from school. Every year we had to cut turf, spread it and get it home. We'd also be seconded to local farmers during the haymaking and beet thinning seasons.

Daddy worked all his life around two places in Rhode — Tokn Grass and Cottons' farm. He had a great wit, though few ever saw it like we did, as he didn't socialise in pubs. Like many of his generation, he was a pioneer all his life.

Other than the family, his two big loves in life were the GAA and Fianna Fail. When he wasn't working to keep the 10 mouths in our house fed, he was either up helping in Rhode GAA, going to matches or helping out for local or general elections.

As my father explained in jest to Mick Lowry, they waited a long time for the family conveyor belt to start working. Two years after I was born, my mother gave birth to their eldest daughter, Mary on April 20, 1953 with Stephen the next boy to be born on December 29, 1954. Eileen came on June 27, 1956 to be followed by Michael on June 3, 1958. Their sixth child was named Seán and he arrived on October 11, 1960. Ann was born on February 2, 1963 and Tomás was the last of the brood, arriving on Christmas Eve, 1964.

Even though there is 13 years age difference between the oldest, myself and Tomás as the youngest, the eight of us Darbys look out for one another. We don't all live in each other's ears but we are there for one another when we are needed.

As Mary was next to me in age, we saw a lot of each other as children and entertained ourselves around the yard and in the house the best we could. Our birthdays are only two years apart. We were always buddies growing up and still are.

I suppose I'd be particularly close to Eileen, who was married to Kevin Farrell, a man who as well as being my brother-in-law, became a really great friend. We socialised together a lot. I still miss Kevin terribly; he was like a brother to me. I can't count the number of times I drove around Edenderry just looking for him to have a laugh and a chat. He was that sort of person. He was a wonderful mimic and in the pub you'd be afraid to go to the toilet because you knew he'd be impersonating you when your back was turned.

Kevin met Eileen first when they both worked in O'Brien's Hardware. They started going out together and then got married. Kevin, who was a couple of years older than me, had a gift for telling stories. It was why he went from being a local journalist to one known nationally through his columns in the Sunday World.

It's hard to believe he is dead six years now. I still miss him as I know Eileen and their three grown up children do. We all miss him.

Of our own clan, Michael is the Darby you don't hear much about from the sporting end of things but he was a good footballer. He played minor and U-21 with the county and was on the Rhode team for a number of years.

Seán also played senior with our club but went to America in '81 to play a match with the Offaly team in the New York championship and stayed on. Although he got the bug for the American lifestyle, he came back to play with Rhode against Walsh Island in the 1982 Offaly final. He was small too but was an amazing competitor and afraid of nothing.

Years and years after that particular final, Richie (Connor) recounted how Seán tried to 'do' him during that game.

The fact that Seán was maybe six or seven inches shorter than Richie made no difference — he would have known the lift other Rhode players would have got if he pole axed the Offaly captain.

Richie had just lifted Sam Maguire the month before. He was popular everywhere but that didn't deter my brother. In the Walsh Island versus Rhode game, the ball came up along the line and Richie went for it leaving himself wide open. Seán saw his opportunity but just as he was about to strike, Richie sensed his presence and changed direction. Seán went whizzing by, just failing to connect by inches.

Richie snapped at him: "You little f**ker, you tried to do me."

Seán scowled back at him: "You were lucky there but I won't miss you the next time."

That was our Seán, fearless. He was a bit like Stephen the way he played — the eyes outside of his head going for every ball. I'll tell you one thing for sure — I'd hate to have had him marking me for a full hour.

Seán has the dubious distinction of being the only man to ever kick Matt Connor on the finger as he prepared to take a 45. Matt was lining the ball up at the time Sean nipped in and stamped on him.

Matt could hardly believe what had just happened and was shaking his hand in pain. Paddy Kerrigan from Rhode, who was over that Walsh Island team, saw what Seán had done and was apoplectic as he shouted into the referee to take action.

While Paddy was in charge of Walsh Island, two of his sons, Benny and Martin Kerrigan were on our team while another, Greg, was a sub. We also had three Darbys playing that day. We were all in the Woof Mooney's on the Monday and in came the Walsh Island team with Paddy in the middle. It didn't take long before he had a go at Seán over the stamping on Matt's finger. When you think of it, there could have been fisticuffs between two Rhode families over a Walsh Island finger but luckily we all managed to see the lighter side of what Seán did and left it at that.

◆ ◆ ◆ ◆

My father was never out of work in his life for a day; now and then he might switch jobs with Tongs and go to Cottons as a farm labourer but he was always in demand because he had a great work ethic. He finished up with the Tongs for the last 25 years of his working life, clocking in for an 8-6 shift every day.

He was very friendly with Paddy Smullen, father of the great flat jockey, Pat. Ironically, Pat now owns most of that farm and has a fine home built on it. I'm delighted to see such a fella do well in life, and the fact that he owns the place his father worked on — a big farm of 400 acres — makes the achievement a little bit extra special.

The Darbys and the Smullens grew up in a time where the children were expected to help out — we were no different to hundreds of thousands of families up and down the country.

What kept me, and others as well, going during all that hardship was the thought that we'd all go up to the field in Ballybryan National School after our supper and play until nightfall.

What was great about those impromptu sessions was the fact that we were playing against lads who were bigger than us... that's where you learnt to mind yourself.

God help anyone who thought they were good and started to show off — they'd be brought down to size very quickly.

We also would cycle up to Fahy Handball alley and the sessions spent there can only have been good for hand-eye co-ordination as well as fitness.

This was the domain of the Mastersons with Pee (Patrick) Masterson and his brother Joe — who is currently president of the handball association of Ireland, exceptional exponents of alley play.

I liked the game though I never really improved at it but Eugene Mulligan was a good hand-baller, as was Johnny Mooney and his brother Thomas.

When it comes to sporting dates, Pee is the go-to man around Rhode because he has a great memory for statistics. If you want to know anything about football, he'll have an answer for you.

The distraction of handball was good because unlike now, there wasn't very much formal football competitions for us when we were in those in-between years. In fact I think I was U-14 when I played my first real match — against Daingean.

The first time I was introduced to regular fare was when I attended the Tech in Edenderry. That's where I played in the first Leinster games of my life, and I loved every minute of it. I was in that school for three years and the highlight was playing in three Leinster finals and one All-Ireland semi-final that unfortunately we lost to a very good team from Antrim.

Even more important from my point of view was the fact that the legendary Galway goalkeeper Johnny Geraghty was a teacher when I was a pupil there. Galway won three-in-a-row of All-Irelands between '64-'66, with Johnny keeping a clean sheet in all three finals. No doubt that was all due to how well we brought him on by taking practice shots at him!

Myself and a couple of other lads would stay on after school some days to make up a practice session for him. He was like a cat the way he could spring around the goal to block our efforts. I was delighted to see lately that Johnny remembered us in an article he wrote for a Galway publication.

In the mid-sixties RTE televised only the All-Ireland semi-finals and final as their full championship package. We used to go to a house which had a telly and we felt so important to see our teacher — the man we practised with during the week — emerge as a hero on the screen on those Sundays.

It was even more special because Johnny was very generous with his time and would talk to us about football, about positioning and about where to place the ball when shooting. He knew what he was on about and we knew that too. We'd listen intently to everything he said — as he highlighted the places where he found it hardest to save shots and where he did and didn't like the ball being put.

He was very encouraging also and if you managed to score a goal on him or do something very well, he would make a point of praising you in front of the others. Imagine how we felt when that happened... it made us try harder to make an impression the next time. I tell you one thing though — you had to work very hard to get any ball past him.

He was part of the reason why football became a bigger and bigger part of my life. From the moment I could walk, I was kicking some sort of ball — usually a burst one — around the yard. Then I graduated to canal bank duty with the cows. I'd always find something to kick up and down the bank after the cows whether it was a tin can or a ball of some description — having something always shortened the journey and turned work into play for me.

Sunday mornings were special because by and large we had the day off — we spent most of it playing football up in Bally-bryan National School where a crowd of up to 20 to 30 players could be involved.

◆ ◆ ◆ ◆

From a young age I was very interested in football. I was never the biggest but I was strong and could win my own ball. And I could score.

That gave me a certain standing both in the Tech with the other lads and in Rhode village because I was a county minor for three years on the trot. I obviously was playing above my age group because although I didn't get a minute's action, I was a sub at 16 on the Rhode team which won the Offaly senior football championship in 1967. That was a particular thrill for me as I sat beside Mick Casey on the bench.

The two Caseys were football legends not just in Offaly but in Leinster and Paddy in New York as well. I had to pinch myself when I had this honour alongside Mick, who was in his forties at that time.

He was finishing his career and I was starting mine. It is still one of the proudest memories that I sat side-by-side with this legendary figure as we both won county medals on the same day.

That team was captained by Paddy McCormack, known universally as 'The Iron Man From Rhode.' Paddy was then, is now and will always be my biggest football hero. The team was full of my heroes with lads who would go on to win All-Irelands with Paddy, Eugene Mulligan, Jody Gunning and Martin Heavey also lining out that day.

I pulled on the Offaly jersey for the first time for Offaly Vocational Schools. We won the Leinster championship that year in 1968 and were beaten in Kells in the All-Ireland semi-final by an Antrim team that went on to win the final.

In the county minor grade, we were beaten by Wexford one year and I can remember distinctly Martin Quigley ran out of Croke Park, jumped into a car and won an U-21 hurling medal later that day somewhere down the country.

Louth and Laois beat us in the other two years I was on the minors. Lads on the Offaly teams I was involved with included Seánie Lowry, Liam Hanlon, Mick Wright, Murt Connor, Paddy Fenning, Tommy Geoghegan, Freddie Grehan, Catch Grennan, Gene Henry, Brendan O'Toole, a very good player from Tullamore and Joe Heffernan RIP.

I won one Leinster U-21 medal and then we were beaten in another Leinster final by Louth. In all I played three years at that level, the same as minor.

◆ ◆ ◆ ◆

My father loved to go to football matches; I heard him talk time and again of cycling to Carlow or Portlaoise to watch Offaly play. He'd follow Rhode to Tullamore and further afield too when they were involved either in tournament or championship games.

In championship, it was win or you're out and that is something I regret to say is lost in the league formats of championship that most counties have introduced over the past three decades.

Daddy loved every minute of every match — it gave him something to talk about it for the rest of the week. Invariably, there would be a flashpoint if someone was sent off, or missed a free or if a fight broke out. This was the fuel that kept the

Christy Darbys of that world motoring; it helped them rise above the drudge of daily hard labour on farms.

Every now and then there was an anti-GAA side to him when Rhode mentors came looking for me to play on evenings we'd be working after he came home from his day job on the farm.

In those situations, he'd hate to see a car pulling up — especially if I was helping him with the grubbing or harrowing after he'd got the loan of a neighbour's pony and would want to get the maximum amount of work done.

On one hand, he'd be very proud if the seniors were looking for me when I was only a chap; on the other hand it meant he had lost a pair of hands for the rest of the evening.

The sixties and seventies were awash with big tournaments running in conjunction with carnivals during the summer months. Often, and this why they wanted me to go, established players would be required for duty either on farms or in Bord na Mona and wouldn't be able to get time off.

Privately I'd rejoice when I'd see Tom Ward, the club secretary with his blue mini, registration EIR 113, pull up outside the field in his car. Tom had a butcher's shop in the village and the GAA was his life — a relation of his, Brendan Ward, would later become chairman of the county board in the eighties.

In my mind's eye, I can still see Tom slowly getting out of his car, climbing up onto the soil bank at the side of the road to look in on us. I'd hear my father curse him under his breath: "What's that f**ker doing here now with all this work to be done?"

I'd point the pony in the direction of Tom, greet him and be over the moon when he'd say I was needed to make up a team that evening.

This was like being sprung from prison. I'd shout down the field: "Tom says they're short tonight for the match and he wants to know can I go, Daddy?"

Sure, what could my poor father do but agree, though I

know full well he'd be cursing me, Tom and the GAA for the rest of the evening as he was left on his own to finish the job.

Tom's car was nearly always packed with players; it meant I'd have to squeeze in somewhere. I'd have jumped into the boot to go — it was a far better proposition to be off to the match instead of working like a slave till dark.

When I think back on it, I'd say Daddy was probably cursing his own situation because he loved nothing more than to be there shouting Rhode on no matter what level of match that was being played.

One such occasion he never missed and neither did any of us, was the seven-a-side tournament in Edenderry. This was massive locally and I can recall crowds of 5,000 in Penthonys Field for the final. They came from the rock and briar to watch Rhode or Ballinabracky or Edenderry themselves or maybe Round Towers of Kildare.

Even before I got involved, I'd go with him on his bike to see the games. I played in a number of tournaments but carnivals and the seven-a-sides were on the decline by the time I was in my prime.

However, the love affair with football was growing; local games to Leinster school fare to county minor to club senior championship. Any big matches I wasn't playing in I was watching and I attended my first All-Ireland final 50 years ago this year when Offaly lost to Kerry in 1969. Daddy and myself went up to it and I remember a lot of the chat before and after the game was the dropping by Offaly of their then captain Pat Monaghan.

That same year, Rhode were back in the winners' enclosure in the Offaly senior championship but it was a close run thing. We beat Erin Rovers (Pullough) in the final and were very, very lucky to do so. The year before Ballycumber had been outsiders but beat Gracefield in the final. Similarly, the underdog led in our game and we were fortunate to draw with Pullough the first day. We then won by a point in the replay.

This was my first active senior final. I played corner-forward. I scored two or three points and naturally as an 18-year-old, I was delighted to have two senior medals at that stage. We were beaten the following year by Ferbane and 1970 also saw Offaly beaten by Mickey Fay, who scored two killer goals as Meath won the only 80 minute Leinster Final on record.

The word was that Offaly threw it away; some said there were too many older players for the length and level of competition. In my own mind, I was thinking it was time I tried to show locally that I should be in contention if new faces were to be considered for 1971 — a year that proved ground-breaking in the history of the county.

We got to the U-21 Leinster final in 1970 and I did well against Wexford scoring 0-3 in the semi-final and was also good against Louth, scoring two points but we eventually lost out by a point 2-13 to 3-9.

CHAPTER 7
LESSONS AND BLESSINGS

Being from Rhode is a blessing if you progress into an Offaly set-up. Back then, it was a big thing to be on the county panel, especially an Offaly senior panel. We grew up on the exploits of teams in the sixties getting to Leinster and All-Ireland finals and in my case, all I ever wanted to do was to be part of that culture.

I was no different to my closest friends Catch Grennan, John Kavanagh and no different to the likes of Seánie Lowry living at the other end of Offaly in Ferbane. He was someone who would share dressing rooms with me all the way up from minor, through U-21 to senior.

During that time, a lot of players came into Offaly squads and didn't have the temperament or background to deal with it. Some got big-headed, some stopped working on their game and others found themselves unable to handle the glare of publicity which came locally from being a 'county man'.

That's why being from Rhode was such a blessing. No one was allowed to get ahead of himself or if he did, he was quickly brought back down to earth.

I'd like to think that I would have come through if I hadn't those people around me who dispensed advice that was handed down the generations on how to behave as an Offaly player. As a young, recent recruit to an Offaly squad, I got a great lesson early on one night in the pub when I was mouthing on about why I should be playing ahead of some other lads in the Offaly forward line.

This was at a time when Offaly was one of the top three teams in the country but had yet to win an All-Ireland. I was still a teenager and was brought into the squad. My fellow Rhode man Paddy McCormack was not just a key player and leader in the dressing-room but doubled up as a county selector as well.

In that time going to county training, there were designated cars — a 'Rhode car' or 'Ferbane car' or 'Gracefield car' which picked up lads from their particular area and drove them to Tullamore or Daingean or wherever the session was being held on a particular evening. You had 'car loads' coming from different parishes — unlike now when most players have their own cars to drive to training.

McCormack had great players like Martin Heavey, Jody Gunning and Eugene Mulligan in his 'load' and on hearing me rise about my station in the pub, he cut me off at the knees in front of everybody.

"Darby," he said in a loud voice, "the only reason you're on the Offaly panel is because I wanted to make up a full load going to training."

That put me in my place I can tell you. From that night on, I knew that idle boasting was not the Offaly way and it taught me to be humble in my approach to football and indeed other walks of life as well.

CHAPTER 8
FINDING MY WAY

I got married at 20; I thought I had seen the world at that stage. I had given up school after getting four honours in the Group Certificate. I should have served my time with Bord na Mona and I regret now that I didn't choose the trade route. Notices were placed in the newspapers but by the time I heard about them, it was a few days too late to apply.

Instead, I got the opportunity to serve my time as a mechanic with Tommy Cullen — a former Offaly great — but had to serve the first 12 months of my apprenticeship attending the petrol pumps at his place in the town.

I remember that my first week's wages was 30 shillings — not much but a small fortune for someone who never had a penny. As time went by, I realised I would be making little more for a number of years serving my time as an apprentice mechanic so I applied for a job in Edenderry Shoe Factory. At that time, that factory was to the town what the Guinness brewery was to Dublin. There were 350 people working there and people felt that once you got in, it was a job for life. My first wage packet was three quid a week... a doubling of the previous money I was on.

I met Veronne Collins, a local girl, when we both were working in the Shoe Factory. Every evening we walked up the street from work together. She'd either wait for me or I'd hang on for her. Our relationship started out as just good friends. At the time she had a boyfriend, but then that ended and myself and herself started going out steady after I brought her to one of the dances in the carnival at the marquee in Edenderry.

We got married a little over a year and a half after we had begun going out. When you look back on it, it was very young but at the time I thought I'd seen and done it all by that stage. After a few years in the shoe factory, I got bored and wanted to try my hand at something else. Reading the local newspaper at home one night, I noticed there was a job advertised for a records clerk in Derrygreenagh in Bord na Mona.

I applied for it the next day, went for an interview a few weeks later and was on cloud nine when I got a letter saying my application had been successful. The job involved keeping records of the machines, the clocking in/out times and maintaining and updating the cards and sheets for employees on a weekly basis.

This is a position I should have stayed in if I was thinking long term. I enjoyed the work immensely but more importantly, I could now be retired out of it with a fine pension. Young people don't think of faraway hills like pensions and I left after two or three years because I was tempted to get out on the road, meet people and as I saw it, make more money.

That was the year I played in the final replay against Kerry in 1972. I upped sticks from my safe job in Derrygreenagh to become a commercial traveller around the roads of Ireland.

This new job involved selling fire extinguishers. In hindsight, this wasn't the cleverest product to be hawking around trying to flog. I suppose I was hoping people would know me after my limited exposure through the GAA but the reality was they didn't.

Naturally I didn't do too well. When you think about it, it is easy to understand why. This was long before fire regulations became mandatory and buying fire extinguishers at the time was seen as something of a real luxury rather than an essential. Nowadays, no business would be covered without them and certainly insurance companies wouldn't pay up if anything happened without them.

I undertook a training course in the company's HQ in Dublin. The boss was a former Armagh footballing great — Jimmy

Whan. He was a good bit older than me but he was very friendly with McCormack and I'd say it was through that connection that I got the job in the first place.

Part of the deal was that I had to provide my own car. Luckily, I had bought one when I got up and going in Derrygreenagh. It made life easier getting to and from work and training.

I had cycled down to the place for the first six months by which time I had put together enough cash, with a little help from home, to buy a mini. The curious thing about that car was that the man who owned it, Lord have mercy on him, was probably 6' 3" or 6' 4" tall and 20st weight. Why he bought a mini was baffling but by the time I got it, the floor was falling out on the driver's side. It was so bad that any time it rained I was almost guaranteed to get out of the car with wet feet.

I'd moved onto a Morris 1100 by the time Jimmy gave me the job — I had gone up ever so slightly in the world with a better car. Nevertheless, I got very little business. I saw the writing was on the wall and got out before I was pushed.

My next venture wasn't a whole lot better — selling tools. This too was a hard slog, though not nearly as difficult as the extinguishers. WJ Ward in Dublin were now my employers and the biggest problem was coming up against the well-known branded names in this industry. The quality of the merchandise I had to offer was good but it wasn't a Stanley knife I was selling, it was an unfamiliar product that wasn't tried and trusted by the consumer.

With my new company Fiat 127 car, I lasted less than a year before throwing in the towel. I was still only 23 at this stage but was already onto the sixth job of my career — this time selling paint. The company was called Synthesis and was located at Woodbine Road in Blackrock, Dublin. I liked this job and it was handier than the previous ones because I didn't have to go to Dublin that often. My week was spent calling around to the shops in the midlands — mostly hardware stores in the big towns.

Obviously, I'd have been known much better through football in this area of the country but once again I was at a distinct disadvantage because what I was selling was a largely unknown brand. It wasn't Dulux or Crown — and they were the names most managers wanted in their shops.

The particular line of paint included very good quality oxides and our price came in a lot cheaper than the big names — so that at least offered some attraction to do business with me. Overall, it was more lucrative than the previous jobs and I was happy to stick with Synthesis for three or four years before deciding to move on again.

CHAPTER 9
MY FIRST COMING (AND GOING)

I was fortunate in some way to have what turned out to be two careers with Offaly. The second part — based mainly around 1982 — most people would know, but first time around, I got called up to the Offaly panel in 1971 before the Leinster Final against Meath. Naturally as a young lad, I was delighted to be part of the journey with such an experienced crew.

I didn't expect to get any game time — and I wasn't disappointed. I sat on the bench for the rest of our games as we won Leinster, the All-Ireland semi-final against Cork and the final against Galway.

I felt maybe I should have got in against Cork but the selectors opted for Daithi Murphy ahead of me. I knew then that I wasn't in their plans and even when things were going badly for a long while against Galway in the final, I didn't entertain any real hopes of being told to strip for action.

The year 1971 was more about getting ready for my wedding than about the game itself. Veronne and I got married the week after the All-Ireland Final on October 2.

That's not to say it wasn't great to be in the Offaly squad. It was. This was the first occasion that the county had won the Sam Maguire and I was fortunate enough to be part of that historic panel. I felt like I'd won the lotto. And while I was grateful for everything, there was something slightly debased about the medal you get as an unused sub, which is what I was. I hadn't really contributed so it felt a little distant for me. Really that year, I was more observer than participant, but happy to be as close as I was to our county's victory.

I wasn't drinking at that stage and as I said, the wedding took priority, so much so that when the squad came back home to Offaly, I didn't go around with the rest of the lads.

Willie Bryan was captain because there was no one starting from the previous year's county champions, Gracefield, although one of their players, John Smith, came on and played a big part in our victory. Willie played for Eire Óg, who were beaten in the final.

The first night the team returned with the Sam Maguire, there was a big reception in his home place, Walsh Island. Two Rhode lads who knew I wouldn't be there got into the function free pretending to be Seamus Darby. That showed that even a short distance from my own home, how unknown I was in GAA circles.

It wasn't until the following year that I finally got the chance to start my first championship game — a Leinster semi-final against Meath. We lined out that day in Croke Park in the Kildare colours and uniquely in my career, I was marked by a man who was smaller than myself.

Mick White was a good one and had won an All-Ireland in 1967 against Cork. I think his last game was against Offaly that day. I cherish the memory of that first game for many reasons, one of which was seeing the late, great Larry Coughlan being filmed before the game kicking shots at goal as part of a movie on Michael Collins.

We won the match by 2-17 to 3-5 on an afternoon when our forwards were outstanding. I managed to get on the scoreboard and did enough to keep my place for the final. That was against Kildare but this time we played in our own colours of green, white and gold and won pulling up by 1-18 to 2-8.

I got a point but was fouled a lot and contributed in that way as Tony McTague stuck over anything from within 40 metres. The downside of that match was the knee injury Nick Clavin suffered playing alongside Willie Bryan at midfield. Nick was on fire that summer in the middle of the park and the sad part from his point of view was that he only had partial use of that leg when he played later in the campaign.

That was a major blow but the squad got a real boost to its hopes of retaining the Sam Maguire cup around that Kildare game when Smith, although not listed among the substitutes, came on for Mick Ryan. He had reportedly "opted out" of the panel and his return was massively welcomed by everyone in the camp.

I played up to the Leinster final and had done enough to retain my place. However I was taken off in the All-Ireland semi-final against Donegal after I came up against Donal Monaghan, the stickiest corner-back of them all as far as I'm concerned. Time and again this man proved my nemesis.

I couldn't get my hands on a ball whenever he marked me and I think there are plenty of forwards of the time who would say the same. Murt Connor came on for me and although he'd agree that he didn't do much better against Donal, he held his place for the final after Kevin Kilmurray scored a clinching goal and we won by 1-17 to 2-10.

I learned a great life lesson that evening after the game. I felt terribly inadequate when I was taken off and it fed into the inferiority complex I had around this Offaly team. I was very shy back then and was in awe of sitting in the same dressing-room as a number of these county stars.

Afterwards, I was on the verge of a group that included Donegal's Brian McEniff, Jody Gunning and one or two other big names. In the course of the conversation, I detached myself more and more from the group simply because I didn't think I had anything worthwhile to say.

I was only married to Veronne for less than a year then but she observed what was happening and called me over to where she was.

"Where do you think you are going?" she asked, and before I could reply she said sternly: "Seamus, go in there and hold your own corner. Your opinion is as important as any of the others."

She was right. In that moment I stopped being ashamed of my performance and did what she said — I went back into the circle and enjoyed the rest of the chat.

I know that Veronne's direction did me an awful lot of good as any time I felt inferior or insecure in a situation afterwards, I just thought of her advice. It was the making of me becoming a proper adult who after that met other people as equals, not as superiors or inferiors.

We were now in countdown mode to play Kerry in the All-Ireland final and I was angry with myself for letting the possible opportunity to start pass me by. I could accept being something of a hanger-on the previous year but now I felt that sitting on the bench was my own fault.

I wasn't the happiest camper watching that All-Ireland final but then the gods threw me a bone when Offaly and Kerry drew 1-13 apiece. Part of me was slightly annoyed I didn't get a run in the drawn game but I was all the more determined to win a starting place for the replay.

From years playing underage together for the county, Murt and myself had become good friends but it didn't stop trying to get the better of each other when it came to an Offaly jersey.

He hadn't played particularly well either in the drawn game and in the three-week run-up to the replay, I pushed myself to the limit and suddenly found a rich vein of form in training. By the time the selectors sat down to pick the team, I knew I was back in the frame.

When I got the nod over Murt for the replay, I was delighted but also a little sad that I would be starting at his expense. It was an unusual looking full-forward line comprising Seamus Darby, John Smith and Paddy Fenning, with Seán Evans switching to play alongside Willie at midfield.

It was said that Kerry didn't lose replays but Offaly had a great team and I didn't buy into that old way of thinking. We knew we were better and all we needed was a bit of luck to win again.

The first half provided us with plenty of luck — but it was the wrong variety — bad luck. We lost arguably the best player in the country that year, Johnny Cooney, to a broken collarbone and before half-time, Eugene Mulligan, the reigning Footballer of the Year, also had to leave the fray through injury. Two big blows and I'm sure fans wondered how we'd cope with such losses against a very mature Kerry side.

I was responsible for Johnny's break in the first 10 minutes of the match. He was on the ground trying to get back up when I accidentally crashed my knee right into his shoulder. I've admitted it to him several times over the years but for a while he was sure I was mistaken and it must have been Paudie Lynch, his marker, who did it.

In the second-half of that game, several things fell into place. Fenning loved the wide-open spaces of Cooney's half-forward position and got on a lot of ball when he moved out. He also scored the only goal of the game with his high, speculative lob deceiving the Kerry goalkeeper, Eamon Fitzgerald, and ending up in the back of the net.

Murt may not have started but he played over an hour's football in the other corner because of Cooney's injury. The day worked out well for all of the younger lads on the panel.

I felt that I did well enough overall. I got out ahead of my man, contributed to the team and kicked two points, one with either foot. I was delighted in the following day's Irish Independent, when the legendary John D Hickey said: "Darby celebrated his first All-Ireland with a capital display".

With every up, there is a down. Shortly after playing in my first All-Ireland final, I got my first serious injury in the league when we played Dublin in Croke Park before Christmas. Their centre-back, Alan Larkin, slid into me as he was trying to get to the ball while I was on the way down hoping to rise it. We collided and I ended up with a broken collarbone. That kept me out of action for three months and when I started to play again, I knew I had a fair bit of ground to make up on the rest of the squad.

*Looking back, I wish I could
have done more than sit togged out
in Croke Park watching the play
from the vantage point of
the substitute bench.*

CHAPTER 10

THE ONE THAT GOT AWAY

That collarbone injury meant I missed several matches early on in 1973 as Offaly set out on a three-in-a-a-row mission. By the time championship season came around, I had failed to convince the selectors that I was back to the standard I'd reached against Kerry in the All-Ireland final replay. I didn't get to start or come on in the Leinster Final where Offaly hammered Meath by 3-21 to 2-12, with Cooney getting 2-2, Kilmurray 1-2 and McTague 0-11 in a forward line that had more than its share of marquee players.

Paddy Keenan lined out at right-half forward and was captain of the team that day. Keenan, Kilmurray and McTague made up the half-forward line with Cooney, Seán Evans and Paddy Fenning inside. That was a competitive sextet to dislodge and I didn't know where I stood until Hughie Healy was brought on ahead of me for Fenning in that game.

That brought it home loud and clear that I had slipped considerably down the pecking order. I didn't get a sniff of action either in the All-Ireland semi-final loss. And so that team failed to fulfil a three-in-a-row of All-Ireland titles which I firmly believe we were more than capable of achieving.

Looking back, I wish I could have done more than sit togged out in Croke Park watching the play from the vantage point of the substitute bench.

Galway played out of their skins against us. I can still see the effortless way the likes of Johnny Tobin and Tom Naughton moved across the pitch. We fought our way back into the game through experience and the pure guts that we had in the team. It was evident though that we were playing a side that was much fresher and more eager to win the ball.

Galway ended up winning by 0-16 to 2-8; late in the game we had a Cooney goal chance and another opportunity for McTague to equalise before Galway broke upfield and their sub, Morgan Hughes, kicked the insurance point in the last minute. Murt got a run for the last 15 minutes for Keenan and that was the only change in personnel made in the forward division.

There was a huge sense of disappointment after that defeat because, as I said already, the team was good enough to complete a three-in-a-row. There was a feeling of having let a very rare opportunity slip and I think that's what hurt most. Personally, I felt marginalised and believed that I could have offered something in terms of scores if I had been used.

That regret may be one of the reasons why I had this sense of unfinished business in the Offaly jersey — so maybe it was a good thing. I had a hunger to succeed and 1972 had given me the appetite to know what it was like to be part of a winning team. I'd had my fill of being a squad player in '71 and '73.

That game turned out to be the beginning of the end for that particular Offaly squad. It was never quite the same force and the rise of Dublin as a footballing power in 1974 accelerated our demise.

That year, I regained my place as we lined-out against Dublin in the Leinster championship. Unfortunately, it also was the day we surrendered our three-year reign as provincial champions. We lost by a point — 1-11 to 0-13. This was Leslie Deegan's finest hour as his score catapulted Dublin out of the doldrums. It was the first significant step on their journey to becoming All-Ireland champions later that September.

They had played two matches before they met us which served them well as they were much sharper and more cohesive than we were. They met Wexford in Carlow and came out on top by 3-9 to 0-6 and then accounted for Louth in Navan by 2-11 to 1-9.

Kevin Heffernan, a man with Offaly blood who became nationally known as 'Heffo', had prepared his squad with a new, ground-breaking fitness regime. Together with the advantage of the two previous games, they were on the front foot for most of their game against us. They went on to beat Kildare in the semi-final and Meath in the final by six and five points respectively.

With those two games in Croke Park, the whole 'Dublin factor' became a thing and by the time they played and beat Cork by six points in the All-Ireland semi-final, there was a force behind them that lasted for the rest of the decade.

They beat Galway by 0-14 to 1-6 in the final with Paddy Cullen saving a penalty from Liam Sammon in front of almost 72,000 in the old Croke Park.

A lot happened between that year's All-Ireland final and the Leinster championship game in which they had beaten us on June 16. We were favourites to win that day. No one in Offaly saw us losing. I watched in disbelief as Deegan, who had come on as a sub for the Dubs, kicked the winning point in the last minute. Seánie Lowry had just made an amazing block but as bad luck would have it, the ball rebounded straight into Leslie's hands and he stuck it over with his left boot.

I remember that day for a few other reasons. I'd had a very good start to the game, saw a shot for goal whiz inches wide and kicked a good point in the first half. I was being marked by the late Dave Billings. Then Heffo sent Gay O'Driscoll in on top of me and he gave me a box and put me into the middle of next week as the two of us contested the first ball that came our way in the second-half. I have no memory of doing too much after that.

That belt hurt but nothing like watching the ball ricochet back into Deegan's arms for the score that knocked us out. If the game had gone to a replay, I'm convinced we would have learned enough from the close call not to underestimate the Dubs a second time.

Sport is often a question of small margins and it is quite possible that had we won that match or a replay, the whole 'Heffo's Army' era could have been stillborn.

There is no doubt we were a team on the turn at that time but on days like that, we showed we could still go head-to-head with the new super powers and not be that far off.

CHAPTER 11

MY BEST YEAR IN AN OFFALY JERSEY

The year 1975 is not even a footnote in my career, yet undoubtedly it was the time I played my best football in an Offaly jersey. I had shown up well in the league where in February we played the new All-Ireland champions, Dublin, in Tullamore. It was like a championship game with a crowd of 16,000 in attendance. There was never more than a kick of the ball between the two teams in a low-scoring game.

The final score was 0-10 to 1-5 in their favour but it took late points from Tony Hanahoe and Jimmy Keaveney to beat us. I never liked the heavy ground but was in really good form that day and kicked a point.

There is no doubt we were a team on the turn at that time but on days like that, we showed we could still go head-to-head with the new super powers and not be that far off.

I thought that even though Kildare and Cork beat us well in the league that year, that the squad was getting its mojo back as we tuned up for championship with neighbours Laois the opposition on June 20.

They hit the ground running and we were out of sorts, though according to one of the local newspapers, I was said to have played my "best game ever for Offaly" that day.

I'd had a major influence, particularly when I moved out to centre-forward where I got my hand on an awful lot of ball. I kicked three points but more importantly really influenced the game after we had gone six or seven points behind. I was happy that I'd played a major part in the fightback for a draw.

There was an off-field row between that game and the replay. It stemmed from a players' protest to the county board that they could not bring their girlfriends or wives to the post-match meal.

This hit the front pages of the national and local newspapers and meant our backs were to the wall when we started the next day in O'Moore Park. Confidence is a great thing in football and that day I felt that I could win every ball. I scored two points while Murt got three goals and we won easily enough by 3-14 to 3-7.

That gave us great lift preparing for the Leinster semi-final against Kildare in Croke Park. We had always been able to handle them in championship and I would have been pretty confident that we would have too much know-how for them.

As it transpired, we hadn't and lost by six points, 2-11 to 0-11. Personally, I did very well again and got two points while also being fouled for several frees which were converted by McTague.

I was nominated for an All Star that year along with Tony, who had previously been honoured on two occasions in '71 and '72. That was as near as I got to that individual accolade and to be honest, I'm a little disappointed that I didn't get it in '75 because I felt like an elite player that year.

It was the first time that I did for Offaly what the likes of McTague, Mulligan, Bryan had been doing regularly over the previous years. I was the go-to player. I don't say that as an idle boast but when the Kildare selectors switched Pat Dunny from their forward line to the defence specifically to mark me, I knew I must have been going well.

Even with a man-marker and recognising how good a player Dunny was, I was on my game and was delighted to get nominated for the All-star. When the awards were announced, Mickey O'Sullivan got the left-half forward slot ahead of me which is hard to argue with given his displays later that year for Kerry while Meath's Ken Rennicks was named at centre-forward, probably the only other place I could have been accommodated.

Not that it would count in terms of All Star consideration, but I carried that summer form through the Offaly championship and was delighted when Rhode ended up winning my third and final Dowling Cup medal.

We ended up beating Daingean by five points, 1-12 to 1-7. In the semi-final, we beat Tullamore by the same margin. I got three points that day but what pleased me most that year was the way I contributed to the team's performance.

Tom Darcy was captain of the side and as was the tradition then, the county champions nominated the Offaly captain and my name was the one put forward and accepted by the county board.

As captain of Offaly, I was being taken off in a championship game. I was crushed. The massive honour of leading Offaly was something I'd cherished but here I was letting down the county, myself and my family.

CHAPTER 12

THE DREAM
AND THE REALITY

I'd like to be able to record for posterity that something good happened under my stewardship as Offaly captain in 1976. The opposite unfortunately was the case; I was taken off in the Leinster quarter-final again Meath in Croke Park and I could have no complaints about the decision.

I had a bad game, full stop. I remember after kicking one of the many wides we accumulated that day, Willie Bryan tore strips off me for not passing the ball to him because he was free. I hadn't seen him because I rushed my shot and it went harmlessly wide. I didn't have too long to wait before I heard the dreaded call from the line. As captain of Offaly, I was being taken off in a championship game. I was crushed. The massive honour of leading Offaly was something I'd cherished but here I was letting down the county, myself and my family.

Even with all the wides, we were still in it until Meath scored two rapid-fire goals after half-time which killed the game off as a contest. We lost by nine points in the end, 3-8 to 0-8.

I was only 25 years old and hoped I might get a second chance to captain the county sometime in the future, feeling as I did, that time was very much on my side.

That day had proved the bulk of the Offaly team from the early seventies was gone. In that situation, it was good to see the minors of that year, Tomás O'Connor, Johnny Mooney, Gerry Carroll, Vincent Henry come along. They would in time step up and help Offaly over the transition period before other young lads such as the two Lowrys — Brendy and Mick — Padge Dunne and John Guinan would come through.

However what we didn't recognise back then was how hard a slog it would be before the county got back to the pinnacle. We'd had a golden crop of players, particularly in that 1971-73 era and I was genuinely blessed to have come along and be part of what they achieved nationally for the county.

Before moving on to my second coming with Offaly, I would like to pay tribute to those players who blazed the trail by winning those first two All-Irelands.

CHAPTER 13

FIRST OF THE FAITHFUL HEROES

As I've alluded to, stepping up to become part of this Offaly squad was a bit strange for me. While I had the ambition to play at the top level, I was rubbing shoulders for the first time with players who were heroes of mine growing up. I had such respect for these men that it was a while before I felt comfortable to talk or offer an opinion in their presence.

Over time, they became my mentors, my colleagues and my friends thanks to a bond that formed in the successful quest to win back-to-back All-Irelands and subsequent failure at the semi-final stage to complete the three-in-a-row.

I think the best way to tell you about that squad is to give short pen pictures of the players who dominated Gaelic football at that time.

Martin Furlong — The man who is the most decorated Offaly footballer of all time. From a minor in 1964 to 1985 when he played his last game for the seniors, he was our last line of defence. (See '82 chapter for fuller profile).

Mick Ryan — What a fabulous player. I marked him quite a bit in training. Very clean, outstanding and got three All Stars. Moved in seamlessly to the fullback position when McCormack retired and got one of his All Stars in his new position.

Paddy McCormack — The most professional GAA player I ever met in his approach to training and preparation for a game. I remember Jody Gunning was suspended for playing rugby with Edenderry and I was put on the frees as an 18-year-old in a championship match. I wasn't consistent with placed balls. I knew that and as a result I was nervous about the game, but more particularly about missing where there was an expectation that it was a simple kick and I should score.

This is where I saw the importance of McCormack's leadership. The very first free we got was out to the right, the wrong side for me, and straight away I was feeling nervous about missing it. McCormack was playing centre back that day and he came up the field shouting and waving: "Heh, Darbs, I'll take that, you go in.".

I did what I was told and he just stroked it over the bar and nonchalantly strolled back down the field as if it didn't cost him a thought.

That was leadership. He was the only one to read my body language and knew as a young lad if I missed it, it might put me off my game for the rest of the day.

What most people don't realise is that Paddy was a good man to score. Often he would end up as top-scorer in inter-firm matches that were big fixtures back that time. In the county final, he was well capable of kicking all the frees but when the next one was a handy 14-yard free, he shouted at me to take it. That was him, all about the team and no ego involved.

He was the same with the county team. Fr. Gilhooley described him as the grand old man of Offaly. To many and I'd be among them, he was Offaly. He was a professional in the way he approached the game and he'd slaughter any of the lads if they stepped out of line. Worse, if you pulled out of a tackle or showed the white feather with a Rhode or Offaly jersey on your back, he'd make mincemeat of you.

You'd be afraid to go into the dressing room at half-time. There'd be no holes barred. I suppose the truth of it was that the other Offaly lads on that team were the same — if you had the green, white and gold jersey on your back and you didn't go for a ball, they'd be queuing up to tell you what they thought of you.

They were a very close bunch that '71-'73 panel. When Mick O'Rourke died this year, they were there to a man. I was one of the younger members of that squad but I saw how that closeness worked in a team and learned from it.

Larry Coughlan — A legend, very inspirational and I loved the way he looked after all the young lads in the panel. He'd come up to you, put his arm around you and make you feel important. He was about 10 years older than I was and many forget that he was a sub on the '61 team.

Larry was a captain in the army and led by example. Certainly, he knew what buttons to press to get me going. He was one tough man, maybe the toughest of the lot. If you wanted to mix it with him, he'd peel you but if you wanted to play football, he could do that as well. His passing evoked great sadness.

Mick O'Rourke — Originally played at corner-forward but then moved back to play left corner back. Obviously he knew how forwards thought and went about making life very unpleasant for them. He was a fully paid up member of the tacklers' union and forwards had to earn every ball they won off him. One of the toughest ever players, he left nothing in the dressing-room. Unfortunately we lost the great St Mary's man earlier this year after a long illness.

Eugene Mulligan — I grew up with Eugene. He was a few years older than me. A great warrior, he never knew when he was beaten. He'd say himself he wasn't the most skilful but he never left anything behind him. Eugene was a great inspiration to anyone playing beside him. When he came out with the ball, he lifted crowds. He was a braveheart and won ball where others would be afraid to put in their hands or boots.

Seánie Lowry — Centre-back in '72 and '82, had the knack of being in the right place at the right time. He played full-forward full-back, midfielder, he could kick frees, he won an All-Star as a centre-back and full-forward. After relocating to Mayo, he won a Connacht title with them before being dropped against Dublin in the semi-final replay in 85. And he was the only player Mayo had with All-Ireland experience. (See '82 chapter for fuller profile).

Martin Heavey — The invisible man of any team who always got the job done. Sometimes lived a little dangerously, but always seemed to be in the right place at the right time. He was only nine and a half stone but if he marked you, you found out how tough he was. A great clubmate who I looked up to in the way he always conducted himself on and off the pitch.

Mick Wright — Came on in '72 for Larry Coughlan on a day when Eugene Mulligan followed Johnny Cooney out of the action, both with broken collarbones. Mick was the original long kicker; I'd say himself and Donie O'Sullivan from Kerry were the longest I've seen. He had great confidence as a player and probably should have been there in '82.

Willie Bryan — A one-off footballer who like all great players always seemed to have time and space on the ball. Himself and Mick O'Connell would have played the game the same way. They suited one another.

As Con Houlihan used to say — and I mean this in the best way possible — they were both fully paid-up members of the non-tacklers' union. They loved going to the clouds and bringing down the ball and they were both very graceful in possession. Neither liked the pulling and dragging that some midfielders before and since would have got involved in.

O'Connell started off well in the '72 All-Ireland final replay but Willie ended up the top man. He gave an exhibition in the second-half and it put him on a pedestal with Offaly fans and I'd say GAA fans everywhere who loved that sort of player — skilful, stylish and graceful.

Seán Evans — Definitely the unsung hero of that Offaly set-up. Seán played full-forward in the 1971 final but manned midfield for the county when needed in '72. Only for him in the semi-final against Donegal, we wouldn't have made it to the final because he switched out and turned the tide in our favour. He was a tireless grafter and as a farmer that was his work ethic. He weighed in with several telling scores during Offaly's glory days in that era.

Half-Forward Line

In the same way that I grew up believing the great Offaly '60-'61 fullback line of McCormack-Hughes-Egan was an inseparable unit, the early seventies half-forward line of Cooney, Kilmurray and McTague was also a blessed trinity.

I've seen many games since that time and nothing can take from the fact that this trio stands up with the very best. You look at the great Kerry team of the seventies and eighties and the Offaly boys were every bit as good as any half-forward line Micko ever put out. I feel the same if you compare them to the Dublin side of the seventies and even the present Dublin team would find it hard to match or better the strength that the individuals brought as a collective line.

Johnny Cooney — There was a time when he was unstoppable and unmarkable playing for Offaly. Mr Perpetual Motion had strength and pace to go past the best of markers. I'd put Johnny Cooney in that same bracket as McCormack in how he trained and prepared for games. Both were outstanding players and gave Offaly an X-factor by their presence in the starting line-up.

In the '69 county final, we played Erin Rovers and Cooney did as much as any one man could possibly do to win the game on his own. We drew with them the first day and were mighty lucky to do so and ended up beating them by a point in the replay.

Kevin Kilmurray — Kevin was powerful, had great stamina and could help out at midfield when we needed it. He also chipped in with some big scores — like the goal against Donegal which set us on our way in the All Ireland semi-final in '72. He was one of the first centre half forwards who knew how to make space for those around him. He was an intelligent man and an intelligent player whose biggest attribute was his ability to keep his team playing on the front foot.

Tony McTague — And then there was this little genius. As with Matt Connor a decade later, I always felt Offaly had a chance of winning once McTague was playing. For a small man, he could win his own ball but he could also go past defenders and draw fouls and set up scores. He had two beautiful feet and his scoring exploits have stood the test of time.

In all honesty during my 60 years or so watching inter-county games, I haven't seen too many better than the Ferbane man. He had everything including a combative nature that made him a nightmare for defenders who thought they could muscle him out of it.

Paddy Fenning — Sometimes Paddy was the other component of that half-forward line and brought different strengths to Offaly when he played out there. He had a great engine, got onto a lot of ball and was always a great team player. He won an Offaly championship at midfield for Tullamore — that's how versatile he was. Wasn't the best man to score but often weighed in with a big one when you weren't expecting it. He'd joke when we meet up that people keep on about my goal in '82 when I was only 13 metres out while there's nothing about his (against Kerry in the second half of the replay in '72) when he scored from 55 metres. My answer has always been the same: "Paddy, there's one big difference between the two goals. Mine was meant, yours wasn't."

Jody Gunning — If we do come back in another life, I'd say Jody will try his hand at being a professional comedian next time around. He was a fella who was always looking for the funny side and he could make people laugh.

He was also a very good rugby player and won a Provincial Towns Cup with Edenderry playing at fullback. Jody was on the team in '71 and on the panel after that and was a brilliant player both on the GAA and the rugby fields.

He was great at getting frees for Rhode and Offaly the way he'd roar and shout if a marker got too close to him. He conned refs for a few years but then they became wise to him, and so did his opponents. They knew they could dish out the hardship and by then referees would very seldom blow in his favour.

The irony of it all was he turned into a very good ref himself and took charge of several county finals as well as some big inter-county games.

He was also successful when he turned his hand to training and was in charge of the Offaly U-21 team in the late eighties that won the county's only ever football title at this grade.

John Smith — This man-mountain made a huge difference when he came on in '71. He could never be accused of being the greatest trainer but once he went onto the pitch, you could depend your life on him. He was a quiet type who loved a battle and in particular if he was playing against Laois, there'd be no stopping him because he lived on the border between the two counties. A great competitor and versatile enough to play really well at centre-back, midfield or full-forward.

Murt Connor — Murt and myself seemed to be always fighting for the same spot on that Offaly team over the three years in a row that we won Leinster from '71-'73 with back-to-back All-Irelands thrown in. He was Offaly's first All-Ireland winning hero for the goal he smashed into the Galway net in 1971. He also played his part the following year and got two points against Kerry when coming in as a sub in the replay. He was in after 10 minutes so got to enjoy it almost as if he had started.

Kieran Claffey (RIP) — A big man who had the mobility to be a great foil to Willie Bryan in the Offaly midfield. He made an All-star of Galway's PJ Smyth who produced a brilliant save from his shot after Kieran's mesmeric run in the '71 final. Didn't know the end of his own strength and a good fella to have in the dressing-room or be with on a night out. Missed out in '72 after remaining in the US following an All-star trip.

Liam Hanlon — Was the third choice midfielder at a time when Willie, Kieran Claffey, Nick Clavin and Seán Evans were also big options. He was in good company and got to play later on in his career.

For all the names that make it in a county jersey, we all know many more who for one reason or another, could have done so but dedicated themselves to other pursuits. **Tony Maher** is one such player and while he was in and around Offaly squads for years, his first commitment was to soccer. Edenderry always had a team of a very high standard competing in Leinster leagues and he was Mr Soccer in the town for years.

Tony and I never got on when we were younger. I was the country boy from Rhode and he was the town slicker from Edenderry. I used to dread having to pass him and his pals whenever I was sent by my mother for messages.

Invariably, they'd be playing soccer on the road and once they saw me coming, they'd make it difficult for me to get past. I recall one day I had a bag of flour on the handlebars of the bike and his gang came after me.

In my haste to get out of the place, the bag fell and there was white stuff all over. I eventually swept most of it back into the bag with my hands and had to make up some excuse to my mother over what had happened.

Tony had a right laugh that day and it was something that stayed with me for years.

I got my revenge — of sorts — in a GAA match. We were both playing for Offaly against Dublin in the Player Wills Tournament at the end of August in 1973. It was a tournament that began that year but never finished because as it happened, Tony came on as a substitute and kicked the equalising point.

Dublin played as if it was a championship game and we had just lost to Galway in the All-Ireland semi-final. Some of our top players were on holiday while others were playing that day against Kerry in Tralee in an All-Ireland U-21 semi-final — which we lost. It meant we had some first team players backed up by the likes of myself who was getting a rare run out that year. Tony was often called up if there was a shortage beyond the normal panel and this was such an occasion.

Shortly after he had come on, I got possession of the ball and he flew past me shouting: "Seamus pass."

He had run into a scoring position and I should have given him the ball. Instead, I just looked at him, remembered my flour incident, and then deliberately turned the other way and passed to someone else who wasn't in nearly as good a position. Tony got one chance and hit the equaliser in that game but as there was no room in the calendar to fit in a replay, the tournament never had a winner.

After my snub during the game, I was sure it would be a case of the two of us being enemies for life.

Four or five years later, my brother Stephen and myself were together in Doyle's Pub in Rhode around Christmas. The phone rang and someone called out: "Seamus Darby, it's for you."

I hadn't a clue who it might be. You could have knocked me down with a feather when the voice said: "Seamus, this is Tony Maher. Listen I've just called the Fire Brigade to your place. I noticed it was on fire as I drove past. I don't think there is too much damage but you need to get over there quick."

Myself and Stephen hopped into the car and were in Edenderry in a few minutes. The firemen were leaving as we arrived and they had kept the damage to a minimum. Tony did me a real good turn that night and I was touched that he bothered to ring the various places around Rhode until he tracked me down in Doyle's.

It's funny how your views change. Since then, we have been best friends. We ring each other several times a week and we know intimate details about our private lives.

Tony is retired as an aircraft technician and manned the government jet for years as part of his Air Corps duties.

He is a great joker himself and likes nothing better than to tell people he played for Offaly in three decades — the sixties, seventies and eighties, albeit just fleetingly as in the example above.

Another good ball-hopper, **Brendy Lowry**, had a way of getting under Tony's skin. Any time they met for a county match, he'd say: "What's that Kildare lad doing knocking around with the Offaly fellas?"

PART II

CHAPTER 14

BACK IN THE OFFALY FOLD

I was on my way to the Faithful Fields lunch on Sunday, May 5th earlier this year when I got a call from James Glennon from Edenderry, who works for RTE, to inform me that Eugene McGee had died suddenly.

Moments later I got another call, this time from Michael Verney of the Irish Independent. We had a chat about how Eugene and myself had been good for each other's careers and he carried a quote about that in the following day's newspaper.

Within minutes, phone calls were being made left, right and centre and once it went on the RTE radio headlines at 11am, there was a huge outpouring of memories from people who knew him in the media or through sport.

Like everyone else, I was deeply shocked because it is indeed true that Eugene and myself were bonded by what happened in 1982. Without taking the chance and bringing me back into the squad and believing in me, I wouldn't have been heard of beyond being a very tiny footnote to the '71-'72 victories. You know the sort of reference: "Seamus Darby was also part of that group."

The goal turned him into an All-Ireland winning manager — something that trumped all his other achievements during his stellar career as a manager.

So, yes, we were good for each other in terms of how we are both remembered from that day against Kerry. In fact, it is not just the two of us but all of the lads from the '82 panel would tell you that only for someone with Eugene's persistence to improve each individual by small margins year on year, Offaly would have fallen short.

I have no doubt about that. And it wasn't just in the way he got us playing to a style that would counter Kerry's strengths, although that too was a factor. It was the way he would make statements which, when I think back on them, were his way of setting goals and making us believe in ourselves. He had the knack of finishing such chats by sounding totally confident that we would achieve our aims.

I have never experienced first hand how Mick O'Dwyer or Kevin Heffernan did the psychological stuff back in that time but I know for sure that McGee was a master at it. And do you know the surprising thing? I didn't even notice what he was doing at the time.

The week after his death, I began recalling some of the one-to-one encounters I had with him once he approached me to go back into the panel in late June, '82.

As is pretty well documented at this stage, he had seen me play in a county championship match against Daingean when I scored a late goal to earn Rhode a draw. After we won the replay, he brought myself and a fine young teenage prospect, Martin Fitzpatrick, into the Offaly panel.

I was coming in off the field in Tullamore after that game on a Friday evening and Eugene approached me and said: "We're having a county squad meeting inside now and you're being invited back onto the panel. I'd like you to come in to it for a few minutes." This was music to my ears and it also had healed whatever rift there might have been between us.

When it comes to fitness, I wouldn't be one of the real dedicated ones like Stephen who kept fit the whole year round. I'd start to get fit in the spring and summer and if Rhode got knocked out of the championship, then I'd let myself go again.

I remember talking to Pat Hartigan, the legendary Limerick hurling defender on one of the All-Star trips in the early seventies about that.

I was explaining to him how I'd start out the year with a bit of a belly on me and would feel great then as I began training and the pounds fell off.

Pat told me he envied me that feeling of measuring and achieving fitness because he stayed the same weight no matter what he ate.

After taking a few months off at the back end of the year, I'd get out at the end of January or early February to begin this process. Often I'd train non-stop from that time until Rhode were beaten in a semi-final in September or a final in October, then it was good to slacken off and enjoy the downtime.

The only trouble for my Offaly career with that sort of thinking was that it allowed me the chance to play myself off the squad every year. Back in the seventies and eighties, the National League began shortly after the All-Ireland final and counties played three games before the Christmas recess and then got a break until the competition resumed in February.

Now I was in no great place to cut a dash in heavy old pitches with the hands frozen off me on miserable and wet October or November Sundays.

Once or twice in the mid-to-late seventies, I might have been on the lash for a weekend and definitely I played some Offaly matches with a few on me. Now I know those who believe the 'Darby and Drink' story will point to this and say: "I told you he had a problem."

The reality back then was that I was no better or worse than most. Indeed I've heard several tales of counties where some players in the sixties had to be taken off because they were hardly able to see the ball after a big Saturday night's drinking session on the way to a Sunday National League game. In other words there was a culture prevalent in those times that wouldn't be tolerated nowadays.

The upshot of those games where I was neither properly fit nor motivated was I didn't make any great impression on Eugene or his selectors. I'd be up for football in the spring if I was approaching a championship match for club or county, but not meaningless games in winter. That's the way my mind worked. I knew that it was my fault that I didn't take advantage of all those times the management were having a 'fresh' look at me.

Yet, I was inclined to blame them more than myself. I felt they could have watched me when I'd be at my best in April or May and when they didn't, I felt I was being hard done by.

It's all the stranger then that while my inter-county career was stalled or seemed to be over, something inside me kept saying that there would be a second coming. That even in my thirties, I would get a call to arms — and then I would take it and make the best of it.

That much had now come to pass with the McGee invitation back onto the panel. I thought I had sufficient motivation to give it a right rattle without Eugene having to say anything. So I was a little surprised when he stood up in front of all the other lads and welcomed Martin and myself in.

"We're adding to the panel tonight lads by bringing in two forwards. None of you need any introduction to Seamus here. He's been around for a long time while Martin is from the opposite end of the spectrum... he's still a teenager and has a lot of talent to bring to the squad.

"There's another reason Seamus is in at this stage of his career — currently he is the best forward playing senior football in Offaly. He also has great experience to bring which will be needed if we are to win the All-Ireland this year."

To describe me in front of the likes of All-Stars like Matt Connor and Brendy Lowry as "the best forward in the county" gave me such a boost that I wasn't going to let him or myself down by showing the white feather during the sessions which were upcoming and which I knew would test me to the very limit.

My first session was the following Monday night on the infamous Clonin Hill. Obviously the other lads had been doing the drills for a few years and were well able for the climb. I wanted to quit several times that night. Togging out, I thought I was fit after training with Rhode for three months or so but this was brutality at a totally different level.

I distinctly can recall making this vow to myself: "I don't care if it kills me, I'm going to keep at it."

These boys around me had lost an All-Ireland semi-final and final in the previous two years and were pushing themselves to unbelievable lengths because they now knew first-hand what was needed. The hill was savage and I could see what McGee had in his head by using it as his central character test — if a person isn't prepared to do this then he's no good to me facing Kerry in Croke Park.

McGee and the lads knew this was no longer just a football game — it was a test of wills. If a fella is bollixed but still refuses to bow the knee — then that's the sort of moral fibre they wanted in the squad. No one failed. Seánie Lowry found the training very, very hard but he stubbornly stuck at it. He just wouldn't let it best him.

I remember the second night I was there — and often the second night is much worse than the first because now you know what's coming — and out of nowhere a young lad who I hardly knew came up to me and whispered: "Keep going, it's great to have you on board."

Then he was off, effortlessly gliding up the hill as if his feet didn't need to touch the ground. Liam Currams is and was a shy person but he will never know the lift his remark gave me that evening.

It energised me. Here was a young lad who had also made his name with the hurlers making sure I felt part of the set-up. These boys had already booked a place in the Leinster Final at that stage of the year so the warm reception they gave to Martin and myself was really uplifting.

They could so easily have had a different attitude — they could have felt: "We've got to an All-Ireland final and are in our fourth Leinster final in a row and these two are being parachuted in out of nowhere."

Never once did we get any resentment. Instead to a man, they made us feel as if we might be the reason they could go all the way. As McGee said: "The stronger the panel, the better chance we have of winning the thing."

Anyway, I resolved that to honour this last chance fate had tossed in my direction, I would leave no stone unturned to get myself as fit as I could possibly be. I'd gone back into Offaly training on June 29 weighing 13st, which would have been pretty much where I needed to be playing club football at the time. The Leinster Final was on August 1 that year and in the three weeks up to the tapering down days before playing Dublin, I worked harder than I ever did before.

I bought a bicycle and cycled five days a week for those three weeks to Rathangan in Co Kildare and back to Edenderry. That was about 20 miles a day and came on top of three pretty hard weekly sessions that Tom Donoghue and Eugene had come up with to have us primed for the Dubs. Not many people realise it even to this day, but those two had made us the fittest team in the country that time — and in the heel of the hunt, that's what beat Kerry.

Inside, there was something blissful happening, despite the drudge of training, during those weeks back in the county fold. I'd always hoped that I'd get another opportunity after being overlooked at the ripe old age of 26. Now at 31 and just when I had almost accepted that there wouldn't be a knock on my door, one came.

The day after I was called back into the panel, I was fortunate to have a first real opportunity to talk to Eugene about what misconceptions each of us may have had about the other since he arrived in Offaly in late 1976.

Daingean had shown the Rhode club and the Darby family remarkable respect by agreeing to shift the game to accommodate Stephen's wedding. The game was originally fixed for O'Connor Park on the day after his wedding — a Sunday, but

In my pram outside the
house in Ballina, Rhode.

Myself and my sister Mary
at the gate lodge in Ballina.

Me, Mary and Stephen playing in Ballybrittan.

Left: My father Christy as a young man in Clonmore.

Below: My mother Janie with Fr Brennan (related to Jim Darby) and my father Christy Darby in a photo taken at the well in Ballina.

My grandfather Michael Gorman, Mamie Darby, my parents Janie and Christy Darby, Alex Tong (in daddy's arms). Granny Gill (our great-granny), Mag Hannigan (Tony's mother), Granny Gorman, Peter Malone (Bill's father). Girl in plaid dress: Clodagh Tong.

The winning Killane team in the Edendery Street League, 1942.
My father Christy is in the middle row, extreme left.

Above: My
parents Christy
and Janie Darby.
Right: Myself
and Mary in
Ballybrittan.

On my Confirmation Day in 1963.

The Rhode Juvenile team which were beaten in the 1966 Offaly Co Final.

Rhode, beaten minor finalists by Clara, 1966.

The 1969 Offaly final was the first senior final I played in, and I collected a winners medal having also collected a medal as an unused sub two years before.

My third and final county senior medal with Rhode was in 1975 after we beat Daingean.

In action for
Offaly during
the 1970s.

Left: At my desk in the office of Bord na Móna in Derrygreenagh, 1971.

Below: Myself, Veronne, Eugene Mulligan and Pat after winning a tournament in Shannon.

Mike and Betty Roche in San Francisco in 1971. Offaly players and the All-Stars all stayed in private houses of people with strong Irish connections. Myself, John Smith and Nicholas Clavin stayed with the Roches. Mike was from Ballylinan, Co Laois and Betty was from Donegal.

On my wedding day with
Seán and my mother Janie.

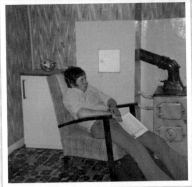

Relaxing in Rochfordbridge shortly
after getting married in 1971.

Myself and Veronne on
holidays in Spain.

Veronne sitting
on the windowsill
outside our shop
in Edenderry.

Anthony Gallagher and Donal Monaghan from Donegal with Sean Evans and myself of Offaly in the 1972 All-Ireland semi-final.

GAA President, Pat Fanning, presented me with my All-Ireland medal in 1972.

Charlie Conroy, myself and the late Eugene McGee. I sponsored bags for the Offaly team in 1981.

The goal that brought the Kingdom down

The Offaly squad of 1982 – Back (l to r) Sean Lowry, Gerry Carroll, Padge Dunne, Liam O'Connor, Dinny Wynne, Liam Currams, Matt Connor, Liam O'Mahoney, Tomás O'Connor, Martin Fitzpatrick and Ollie Minnock. Middle – Mick Fitzgerald, Pat Fitzgerald, Martin Furlong, Richie Connor, John Guinan, Johnny Mooney, Brendan Lowry, Mick Lowry, Charlie Conroy. Front – Stephen Darby, Hugh Bolton, myself and Aidan O'Halloran.

The 1982 All-Ireland final programme (left) and the week after the final I was named Sportstar of the Week in the *Irish Independent*.

Hello Sam. At last an Offalyman gets his hands on the Sam Maguire. Willie Bryan (above) holds the cup aloft as players and officials celebrate. Below: Sam arriving in Edenderry in 1982. In passenger's seat at front is Brendan 'Locks' Kelly. Behind Sam Maguire is Dr Brian Emerson, team doctor, Paddy Fenlon (selector), myself, Padge Dunne, John Guinan (at the back) and local Deputy Ger Connolly.

In my office in Derrygreenagh with Sam.

Previous pages: Being carried off the Croke Park pitch with Johnny Mooney after the victory over Kerry.

Myself with Eugene Mulligan, Jody Gunning, Martin Heavey and a group of supporters celebrating at a dinner dance in London.

they gave the county board permission to fix it for the Friday night.

The following day I was Stephen's best man and his wedding was an immensely enjoyable function for many reasons. In terms of my Offaly future, I was getting the chance to sit down with Eugene in the Royal Hoey Hotel in Athlone to talk out our grievances.

For instance, I knew he would not have been that impressed when he gave me the opportunity to play in early league games that I wasn't in great shape or indeed might have looked as if I was going through the motions. I think I might have played one game a year on the strength of my reputation and earlier form with Rhode in '77, '78 and '79 and that was it.

He said it was true that I hadn't shown anything special but he was convinced after watching me over the previous two weeks that I could be a real addition if I worked hard.

We agreed to let bygones by bygones and I told him I had no intention of simply going along for the ride at my age.

"I want to make a difference so Offaly can win the All-Ireland this year," I told him.

I could see he was impressed.

He then told me that there was the possibility of a starting place because Vinny Henry had gone up to Donegal to work as a Custom's Officer. He said Vinny had been a very valued member of the squad. He explained that he often did a lot of unseen work that might not be appreciated by the supporters but the other forwards knew how good his movement was in creating space for them.

I would have seen myself more as a finisher than a creator in the Vinny mould and told him that up front. He explained that the Offaly forward division was about teamwork and not individuals and he saw from how I made scores playing for Rhode that I would be able to do the same at inter-county level. I think he also mentioned that he had no objection if I came up with the odd important score myself but he wanted me to be more than an out-and-out finisher.

Quite rightly, he pointed out that Matt and Brendy were already pretty good in that department. It was about balance, he maintained, and while not guaranteeing me a place on the team, he felt that if I made it to the starting 15, that I would enhance the sort of balance he was seeking.

The curious thing about that conversation was it would never take place nowadays. Here we were four weeks out from a Leinster Final and we had three or four drinks as we discussed how I might fit into the Offaly team that had already beaten Louth and then Laois in the Leinster semi-final.

Eugene liked a social drink himself and was never one for having vigilantes operating across the county telling him who was or wasn't drinking at any stage leading up to important matches. He knew what lads to keep an eye on and he only ever mentioned drink as a way of telling us to be responsible in choosing when we took one.

That same day, lads from the panel at Stephen's wedding were drinking without fear of being admonished by their manager or indeed by the other Offaly people attending the celebrations.

What that time in each other's company did for both of us was incalculable. A trust formed. I wanted to get across to him how much of an honour playing for Offaly was to me and how up for the challenge I was. What I heard back clearly from him — which was really important to me — was that if I performed well in the challenges games he had organised, there was a possible place there for me.

I had a slight issue with the role he wanted me to play. It wasn't my natural game but I was so hungry to make it I decided if that's the plan he had, then who was I to argue? In retrospect, that conversation changed our relationship totally. Whatever issues that might have been in each other's minds were firmly put to bed.

Shaking hands as we parted to go mingle with other guests, I was already pursuing an 'operation comeback' in my head. That was when I got the idea to buy a bike and pursue my own new level of fitness. It was half a dozen years since I played championship football and I hadn't exactly covered myself in glory that day against Meath. I wanted to give my family a different memory now that I had the chance and I'd move mountains to see if I could achieve that.

Between my own cycling sessions and the Offaly physical stuff, I trained in the following weeks like I'd never trained before. I was lucky that I was coming in off a decent enough base from the Rhode senior squad, but the intensity of those sessions was on a level that tested me to the core.

By the end of the first week I was feeling great; not only was I getting through each session but in a perverse way I began enjoying them. I knew they would sharpen me up and help me play better when I got my chance.

That arrived quickly. On the Sunday of that first weekend, we played Westmeath in a challenge game in Durrow, on the Offaly-Westmeath border, between Kilbeggan and Tullamore.

After what Eugene had said at the wedding, I was hoping to get a half to show what I could do. When the side was called out in the dressing room I was picked at full-forward. I wasn't expecting that either as most of my best games came in the corner-forward position. If he had called my name to play in goal, I wasn't going to complain. It may have only been a challenge game, but it felt great to be back.

Westmeath were already out of the Leinster championship by that time in early July but their county board obliged us by fielding a strong team. They had played three games in that year's Leinster championship, beating Wicklow in a replay and then putting it up to a really good Laois team in mid-June before finally losing by 2-9 to 1-7.

So they would have been still fairly fit by the time we played them and McGee looked on it as a decent test to keep us ticking over. Ideally, he wanted a good workout and then it would be good for our confidence if we pulled away near the end.

I think Sean Tone played full-back on me that day and while I didn't set the world on fire, I was happy that I did what Eugene wanted. I got out in front as often as I could, I sprayed the ball around to the danger men and we won. I was a bit unhappy that I only scored a point but then I'd naturally feel like that. I needed to score two or three times per game to reach my own standards. Only then would I come off the field feeling happy. He introduced me to the "roving full-forward" concept and I enjoyed the quality of movement around me. You could see the intelligence in the runs being made and all I had to do was flick the ball around for scores to come.

In that time of knockout championships, people's interest was concentrated — there were no second chances. There was also a phenomenal interest in a county team if it was going well and clearly Offaly were. Those challenge games drew big crowds and you'd have the situation where a lot of people would turn up to watch us in training before a big match like a Leinster final.

So the word spread around Offaly that Seamus Darby had been recalled to the panel, and naturally not everyone thought it was a good move. I can understand that given my age but by bringing Martin Fitzpatrick and myself in on the same date, it went down a lot better than if it was just myself.

I didn't really care what people thought, though it was nice to see the number of genuine fans I met who wished me well. My father especially was delighted — he now had two sons on the Offaly panel.

It was still full on in training and my body had never felt so tired after those sessions; but a good sort of tiredness. I slept like a log and woke up feeling stronger than I ever did.

We went down to play Cork in Fermoy the following weekend. McGee told us he had arranged a Saturday evening game and he wanted it to be a real test. Cork had drawn 0-9 each with Kerry in Páirc Uí Chaoimh early in that month of July and like ourselves, they were looking for a good game to keep them in top shape for the Munster Final replay against Kerry. That didn't take place until August 2, which obviously we know from history that Kerry won.

It was hardly a surprise then that the match between Cork and ourselves had more than a bit of championship fervour about it. I had a really good day against one of the finest full-backs of that time — Kevin Kehilly.

He had done well against the 'Bomber' by holding him to a point in the drawn game and in his career won two All-Stars, one of which he earned that year in a full-back line of Mick Fitzgerald, Liam O'Connor and himself (he was picked in the corner).

On the bus as we made our way back to Offaly, I was delighted with the way that I had brought other forwards into play. I think I might have got a point that evening but my own view was that I should be contributing a lot more in the scoring stakes. Having not done that for two games, and despite playing really well, I dropped my own expectations of playing against Dublin in the Leinster Final.

As the players chatted among themselves on the journey, the consensus was that it would be the week of the Leinster final before the team was announced. Everyone knew more or less what the team would be except for the one place in the forward line created by Richie's knee injury that necessitated Seánie Lowry reverting from full-forward to centre-back.

We pulled into the Cashel Kings Hotel in Tipperary for food — a place that is long since gone. We had our meal and got back into the bus for the rest of the journey back.

We hadn't travelled far when McGee stood up in front of us and announced that the selectors and himself had picked the team to play Dublin and had decided to tell the panel well in advance.

He called it out as follows — Martin Furlong in goal and

captain; Full-back line: Mick Fitzgerald, Liam O'Connor and Mick Lowry; Half-back line: Pat Fitzgerald, Seánie Lowry and Liam Currams. Midfield: Tomás O'Connor and Pádraig Dunne. Half-forward line: Aidan O'Halloran, Gerry Carroll and John Guinan. Full-forward line: Matt Connor, Seamus Darby and Brendan Lowry.

As he named the subs, I was still aware of his voice but didn't hear what he was saying. All I could think of was that I was in the team for the Leinster Final. I was shell-shocked.

Eugene then made a few points about the importance of getting over Dublin but very little else sunk in with me. My mind was in a bit of a haze for the rest of the journey home.

When you're younger as I was back in '72, there is a youthful arrogance that you expect to play as I did for that replayed final. The older me hadn't such presumption but I was one happy man to be back in the championship fold.

When it came to his approach to upcoming matches, Eugene had a unique way of thinking. In the time of knock-out championships, there were often long periods between games and his method was to get a team to focus in a month or so in advance. So he'd tell his players their next opponents were "six or eight points a better team if the game was to be played right now".

Years after we'd beaten Kerry in '82, I saw where he'd written that when Offaly had lost by seven points in '81, his plan was to improve the team by nine points. Obviously he wasn't quite spot on as we won by a point not the two he had trained for.

That was a technique he evolved to make the countdown weeks important. He applied something abstract, got a buy-in to his concept... resulting in players' concentration for an upcoming match improving immeasurably as a result.

Lads who were in under his wing would tell you that such a simple mechanism worked wonders for their application in those long run-ups to games. It kept them focused on trying to be the best they could be so that when the ball was thrown in, they'd already be convinced that they had done the work and there could only be one outcome.

As I think back on this time, I believe Eugene decided to pick that Offaly team with me in it a few weeks ahead of the Leinster Final to give players the chance to become familiar with those new faces they had alongside them in defence and attack.

Don't forget, he had taken the calculated gamble of omitting Richie so that his knee could be operated on in time to be back for the All-Ireland semi-final, and final, if we got that far. Seánie was then brought back to No 6 in Richie's place and I was drafted in from outside the panel, in many respects, to be the fulcrum of the forward line.

Doing that in the week of a final could unsettle a team, not to mention supporters. By announcing the starting 15 so far out, we got used to the selection in the training sessions so that by the time we took to the field in Croke Park against Dublin, there was nothing knew about the team for any of us.

Eugene wasn't a man who needed to talk to the group every night or indeed to individual players on an on-going basis. But when he did have a little chat with you, it mattered.

From the time the team was announced, he pulled me aside a few times just to let me know that he was convinced I would make a huge difference against Dublin. He told me to take my chances if they came but to remember my playmaking role as we had two of the deadliest finishers in the game either side of me.

There is no denying he was 100 per cent correct in that assessment but all the while he was telling me this, the stubborn voice inside my head wanted to show him that I could finish too if I got the opportunity.

So whether he contrived it in such a manner or whether the suggestion was unintentional, I knew I was going to show him and everyone else that Darby could score as well as make scores when we played Dublin.

This was a crisis moment. I'd never had a hamstring injury before so I didn't know that I should go off immediately. Instead my first thought was to see if I could nurse my way through the rest of the game.

CHAPTER 15
A COMEBACK TO REMEMBER

While Dublin were nothing like the machine of the seventies in the early eighties, Offaly supporters were wary of playing them in a final, particularly as the loss of Richie was, psychologically, a blow for us and a boost for them.

If our fans had been told in advance that Padge Dunne would have been injured after 20 minutes, then those among the 32,504 crowd in Croke Park that day would have travelled with even less expectation of a victory.

Yet the manner in which the team tackled such adversity on the day and emerged victorious against Kevin Heffernan's side by 1-16 to 1-7, if anything, gave everyone a lift that the team was still on the up, particularly when the return of Richie from injury and Johnny Mooney from America could be factored in for the remainder of the series.

The local newspapers gave Eugene and his selectors the kudos for how they handled the situation and the leadership they showed in getting the best out of the talent available. The late Eddie Rogers in the Offaly Independent put it this way: "The contribution made to Sunday's victory by team manager, Eugene McGee and his fellow selectors deserves to be recognised and acknowledged.

"Faced with the need to provide experience and maturity to replace Richie Connor's leadership at the heart of the defence, they took the rather obvious step of restoring Seán Lowry to centre-half back and the less obvious decision to recall Seamus Darby from inter-county oblivion to plug the gap thus left in attack.

"This was a bold move that met with less than general

approval but on the day, the wisdom of the selectors was more than vindicated as Lowry and Darby both rose to the occasion to emerge as huge successes in their allotted roles.

"Impressive though Lowry was, he must take a back seat in the honours list to Darby who proved all his critics wrong by his lively performance at full-forward — a position that has been a recurring trouble spot for Offaly in recent years. Full of zest and cunning, he gave the Dublin defence a roasting, first taming Tommy Drumm and then dealing with equal effectiveness with Mick Holden.

"There was simply no curbing the 31-year-old Rhode man who belied through his performance his six years absence from championship football. He pointed the way with the opening score after only two minutes but his most telling contribution was the 21st minutes goal that really put the skids under the Dubs.

"Darby in all scored 1-3 and in a day when both Matt Connor and Brendan Lowry lost their scoring flair, this was sufficient to make him top-scorer in the final, a distinction earned in the immediate preceding year by Brendan Lowry (1981), Matt Connor (1980) and Seán Lowry (1979), the first time in 50 years that one county has provided the top scorer in four successive finals."

There were portents of things to come too for Martin Furlong, playing in his 10th Leinster Final that day. He led from the back and his form was on a par with his courage. The point was made that the three star performers on that day were from the '71-'72 era.

However, I wasn't one of those who cared anything about past glories; I wanted more than anything to help write a new chapter for Offaly football — and this win was a step in the right direction.

What wasn't known by the local or national press or indeed the other players on that day was that I had injured myself just before half time. After the first half I had played, I was feeling really good and felt I could win every ball kicked in my direction.

Tommy Drumm had been switched off me and Mick Holden had slotted in beside me at full-back. I wanted to get out ahead of Mick for that first ball between us. I sprinted with all my might and was ahead of him when I felt my right hamstring tear.

This was a crisis moment. I'd never had a hamstring injury before so I didn't know that I should go off immediately. Instead my first thought was to see if I could nurse my way through the rest of the game without anyone knowing it had gone — and that is precisely what I did.

Even at half-time, I said nothing to the medics in our corner other than asking them to bandage up my thigh as I wanted a little support there.

My thinking was — if I can get through this, I'll have time for the injury to heal by the next game. Luckily I had done my scoring in the first half as I did very little after that. No one seemed to notice that I had an injury and I was happy with that. When the final whistle went, there was joy that we had won so comprehensively but by that stage, Offaly eyes were on a bigger prize than a provincial title.

As Furlong was collecting the Leinster Cup, I began to wonder if I would miss the All-Ireland semi-final three weeks down the road.

If it was today I know what would have happened in such circumstances — I'd have come off once I felt my hamstring go. No bravado, no stupidity. The injury would have been iced and as the tear was only halfway up under my arse, it would have had plenty of time to heal.

It was part of the general thinking then that hamstrings were new fangled injuries which no one ever suffered until cars arrived in the country. There was no scientific understanding by me of what harm I was causing myself by staying on, so stay on I did.

I was cheered up in the dressing-room by the players' reaction to how I had played, even when I was trying to protect my injured leg all through the second half.

It wasn't until we reconvened on the Tuesday night for training in Ballycommon that I told McGee what had happened to me during the game.

With that sin of omission finally off my mind, I cheered myself up that I was a quick healer. I figured I had good powers of recovery and felt that if I rested my hamstring for a few weeks, I'd be fine.

Eugene told me the selectors and himself were very happy with how I had performed and as far as he was concerned, I had brought experience to the forward line which would be needed if we were to go all the way. He set me up with a local physio and told me the selectors and himself would put no pressure on me. However, they would have to be sure that I had recovered fully from the hamstring as the last thing they wanted was to have to replace me five minutes into the Galway game if it went again.

I understood that perfectly and decided I would do everything in my power to speed the recovery process.

CHAPTER 16

GALWAY — WHY I
WASN'T AT THE RACES

Our All-Ireland semi-final was fixed for Sunday August 22 and initially I estimated that I would be ok the week before and would pass a fitness test if one was required on the eve of the game.

But things went better than I'd anticipated. By the Thursday week after the Dublin game, I tried a few runs and I got no reaction from the hamstring. I was confident that I was fine again. Of course, I should have had enough sense to be cautious; to stick to straight-line running that week and then to start going flat out three or four days before the Galway match.

When so-called adults put on their training kit, something strange happens — they become little boys again. Certainly that was the case with me. The following day after doing the running, I was giddy to start kicking the ball. So on the Friday evening training spin in Ballycommon, nine days before the All-Ireland semi-final, I told myself that a few shots on Furlong would do no harm.

It had been a particularly fine day but a heavy shower arrived about an hour before we went out on the pitch, making the grass very slippery. If you were one of the lads who arrived early for training, one of the pluses was getting the opportunity to do a bit of shooting practice. It reminded me of playing with the lads I grew up with in Rhode; throwing down two jumpers and one of us would go in goal and the others would think we were Cyril Dunne, Charlie Gallagher or Sean O'Neill taking shots. Those little sessions are probably why I loved football so much.

Matt was always one of the first to arrive and he'd mix kicking frees with picking up a ball and soloing through and aiming for a goal in the corner. Brendy was always tweaking his way of shooting and fellas further out the field in games like Gerry Carroll and John Guinan would also love these mini-sessions.

I did a few short runs between the end line and the 21-yard-line to warm up and then the temptation to get involved proved too much. They were taking shots on Furlong and his deputy Dinny Wynne — one would try to save a shot and then step out to let the other face the next kicker.

I hit a few easy shots and felt nothing so my confidence rose. I kicked one or two more a bit harder and everything was still fine. Then I fastened onto a pass from one of the boys further out the pitch. I jumped slightly to collect it and as I was about to take a shot my standing foot gave way and I felt the pull straight away on the other leg.

I knew I was in deep, deep trouble now as time was against making a recovery with nine days left to throw in.

In my efforts to play, I asked Eugene if he knew any physio who would work on me twice a day if necessary to speed up the recovery. Someone had gone to Amy Johnson in Blanchardstown up in Dublin before and he dug out a phone number for me to ring.

I rang her that night and left a message and even though the following day was a Saturday, she rang me back and I drove up that day for what became eight days of virtually non-stop treatment.

It involved driving up and down from Edenderry for an early morning appointment and then coming back for another in the evening as well. In between I was trying to do at least part of a day's work between the driving up and down. I couldn't afford to hang around Dublin and waste a full day just waiting to go back in for the second bout of treatment.

Coincidentally, Kerry's Jimmy Deenihan was also being treated by Amy at the same time. We sometimes bumped into each other going to and from sessions. Jimmy had broken his ankle in an in-house match between the Kerry panel the previous month and Micko knew his value as a defender and was hoping to get him back for the final.

I think they all were experienced enough to know it was a long shot as again the clock was against him to be ready after such a break. I'd say he had it in his head to do everything he could to tog out and be there if he was needed.

The irony of the two of us using the same physio to get fit; one of us — me — would be back in time for the final while Jimmy ran out of time. I know many people, particularly Micko, felt that if Jimmy was corner-back in the '82 All-Ireland final, there would have been no Darby goal and consequently a totally different outcome to the game.

Word by now had got out to the newspapers that I was in a race against time to line out for the Galway match. As promised, the selectors gave me to the eve of the game to prove my fitness. The optimist in me — and I'm blessed with a lot of that — started to whisper that these twice daily sessions might get me across the white line for the game.

I also have a streak of realism inside me which told me that no matter how often I got treatment on a hamstring injury, nine days would never be enough. It was no use to anyone if I thought negatively like that so my aim was to confound medical opinion and make it.

Eugene and his management team went along with me. They picked the team for the programme and had me listed at full-forward for the game.

They made changes from the Leinster final with Richie picked to play at midfield alongside his first cousin Tomás. Padge was moved as a sort of third midfielder to right half forward while Johnny Mooney would replace me if I failed the fitness test on the edge of the square.

Everyone in Offaly, myself included, was delighted that Mooney was back. As a fellow Rhode man, no one needed to tell me what he could bring to the plate as I'd seen what he could do since he was a young lad in short trousers. He was different class — great hands, the spring of a gazelle and blessed with the accuracy of a forward when by inclination he was a mid-fielder. On top of all that, he was a warrior — afraid of nothing and would bring a physicality that meant even if his man got the ball, he had a job to get past him. It has often surprised me down the years how people have failed to recognise his impor-tance — without his vision, ability to create space and desire to win — I don't think we'd have won the All-Ireland that year.

Never mind the final, we wouldn't have got out of Croke Park as winners in the semi-final. We played Laois in a challenge match on the Sunday before playing Galway and Mooney lined out at full-forward in my place. News that he had arrived back from America a day or two before the challenge match drew a big crowd to Tullamore, where against an understrength Laois side, who needed four of our subs to complete their team, Offaly won easily by 5-15 to 1-7.

Given the length of time he was in the air travelling from San Francisco to get home, Johnny arrived into the dressing-room complaining of a terrible headache. He played for the 70 min-utes and still didn't feel great after the game. Despite this and the fact that he hadn't been playing anywhere approaching this level while living in the States, he was our stand-out play-er. Class is certainly permanent in his case as headache or no headache, he was out in front for every ball, making score after score with his clever use of possession. The biggest cheer of the day came when he kicked over a point to cap a fantastic display.

I was genuinely delighted for Mooney but also recognised that his form had implications for me — particularly if I didn't make it to the starting line up. Like many others around Offaly GAA, McGee had always claimed that we would need Mooney to win the All-Ireland.

It certainly would have given the selectors a major headache if I had passed the fitness test the day before the Galway game. What would they have done? Drop me after scoring 1-3 and playing well in the Leinster Final or hold Mooney in reserve?

It never got to that. Despite my best efforts, I was unable to sprint flat out when I tried the hamstring. That settled it — Mooney would be in from the start.

As it turned out the team that started against Galway would be the same 15 who lined out against Kerry — but McGee made five positional switches. For the Galway game, Gerry Carroll stayed at centre-forward but would switch to the wing for the final, Richie would move up to the 'forty' and Dunne would revert to midfield while Matt would swap the left-half forward slot for the No 14 jersey between those games. John Guinan started the Galway match at full-forward but would do Trojan work at left half forward against Kerry while Mooney would switch into the No 13 jersey for the semi-final and stay there for the final.

They say that semi-finals are there to be won and that was about the best thing that could be said about Offaly against Galway. It was an overcast and windswept day and the standard of football was not out of the top drawer. It was a dour game with little or no bright patches.

I didn't tog out but I put on a tracksuit and went with the rest of the lads into the dugout and watched the game like all the Offaly spectators, wondering when would we click into gear and play like I knew we could.

Somehow we managed to win ugly but we were all on tenterhooks for the last 10 minutes or so because the winning of it was there for Galway if they had taken their chances.

They won the toss and elected to play with a fairly whimsical breeze for the truth was no one knew which team it favoured. At half-time, we were only a point down and the expectation was that we would go on and win it from there.

For me three things stand out from that game — Mooney's man of the match performance, Richie kicking the winning point with eight minutes plus injury time left on the clock and then how slowly time passed at the end when Galway camped in our half trying to get the equaliser.

We were hanging on for dear life and luckily for us they spurned two or three really good chances to force a replay. The most popular man from an Offaly point of view in Croke Park was Weeshie Fogarty when he blew the final whistle, as it happened a few seconds short of the full 70 minutes. No one in Offaly was complaining.

Certainly, the Offaly fans in the 25,111 crowd at the game rejoiced that we had made it to our second successive All-Ireland final but the truth was we had given our worst performance since the previous year's final.

A number of our big names had poor games and really only for Mooney, we wouldn't have been at the races. "Without doubt, Offaly's man of the match was Johnny Mooney, who lined out at right full forward, with John Guinan moving into the centre when Seamus Darby failed to satisfy the selectors regarding his total fitness," stated the Tullamore Tribune.

It went on: "Mooney fully justified the expense incurred in flying him home from the States for to put it bluntly, his presence represented the difference between winning and losing on Sunday. Until understandably tiring in the very late stages, the Rhode man menaced the Galway defence with a co-ordinated exhibition of high fielding, physical toughness and astute distribution. All this with the minimum organised preparation, which holds out bright promise of an even sharper performance in four weeks time."

Yet many left Croke Park that evening despondent that on that showing, we wouldn't keep the ball kicked out to Kerry in the final. McGee did little to prevent journalists from thinking along those lines by declaring on the front page of the Irish Independent that Offaly had no chance in the final and added mischievously that they mightn't even bother turning up for the game.

In retrospect, the way the semi-finals unfolded couldn't have been scripted better from an Offaly point of view. And it helps you understand why those lads in Kerry got the five-in-a-row songs and t-shirts done in advance.

Offaly were all but written off by neutrals and Kerry, looking in at that match after trouncing Armagh in the other semi, wouldn't exactly have been quaking in their boots.

There was another contributing factor to that Kerry superiority which helped Offaly big time — though we didn't know it then — how the referee saw the game.

The late Weeshie Fogarty was a hugely respected figure in Kerry GAA circles and the verdict he brought back to the Kingdom on the match he had just refereed was that Offaly wouldn't pose a major threat.

Writing in the Kerryman newspaper in 2005, he assessed what he had seen from his bird's eye view on the pitch as follows: "I had more than just a Kerry interest in this particular final. Only weeks previously I had refereed the semi-final as Offaly beat Galway. Not a great game by any means. Offaly fell five points down at one stage, but came back to snatch it in a thrilling finish. The one thing that I vividly remember about that game was Offaly's patience and slow build-up and Sean Lowry and Johnny Mooney continually urging their team mates with words like 'don't rush it, take your time' and 'don't give away the ball.'

"This tactic was to prove decisive in the final shortly after. I had also refereed some of Kerry's trial matches in the build-up to the final at the request of Mick O'Dwyer and there was nothing to suggest that this great Kerry team would not win the near impossible five-in-a-row of All-Ireland titles. Unlike Offaly, Kerry easily beat Armagh by 10 points in their semi-final on a 3-15 to 1-11 scoreline."

Without actually banging a drum about it, Weeshie's judgement would have added to the already runaway feeling that Kerry were home and hosed before a ball had been kicked.

When all of those factors were taken into consideration —
Kerry's easy win, our below par performance and the fact that
Weeshie had witnessed first hand how poor that showing was,
it was hard for the Kingdom not to expect to create history by
winning on September 19, 1982.

There was a long run-up of four weeks to that date for us
and while the concern for most people was to get tickets for the
game, mine was to get fit again so that I could at least present
myself to the management team as an alternative on the day. I
knew realistically that was as much as I could hope for, given
how the semi-final had gone.

CHAPTER 17

THE FINAL COUNTDOWN

After returning to fitness I had no expectation of winning back my place in the starting line-up. The way Mooney had played in the semi-final meant he was a certainty to start and with Richie being pushed into the forward line to do a specific job on Tim Kennelly, there weren't too many places going a-begging at my end of the field.

The full-forward line of Johnny, Matt and Brendy was rightly a closed shop with Matt operating at full-forward. While Gerry Carroll had been inconsistent for much of the year, he had the class to turn a game and his record against Kerry was good which meant Richie and himself were automatically pencilled in on the half-forward line. That left just one position and as Padge had at last been picked in his favourite midfield slot alongside Tomás O'Connor, it meant the number 12 jersey was probably the last one that a few panellists felt they might have a chance of claiming.

In my opinion, McGee and his selectors made the right call by choosing John Guinan to start. This guy was a find for Offaly when he came into the squad the previous year and he brought toughness and work rate which would be needed to complement Richie in keeping those Kerry backs from straying too far up the field. The two boys did their job magnificently on the day and though Páidí escaped Gerry Carroll on the other side to get two points, I think the Edenderry man earned his corn by finishing strongly when switched out to midfield.

As everyone knows at this stage, I went in for John with seven minutes or so remaining and while he didn't score in the final, that was never his primary job. He had been detailed to physically form a barrier with Richie to stop the Kerry half-backs making their sallies up field and he certainly did that.

One of the clearest images I can still recall from the game is Richie stopping Kennelly in his tracks as he tried to come out with the ball in the first half. He actually lifted him into the air with the force of the impact. No sooner had he done that with all his physical might than Guinan met the great Kerry defender from the other side with an equally ferocious but fair thump.

Most players at the receiving end of such a double blow would have been out for the count after that. All I can say is Kennelly was some man to keep going, having shipped those two belts. I think it's fair to say he hadn't anything like the impact on that game that he had on the one 12 months before.

That was the sort of shift McGee had insisted Offaly needed to put in if they were to be there or thereabouts when the game was entering its closing phases. He made the point that Kerry were seldom brought to the wire in Croke Park during their great run. He drilled it into us that he wanted Offaly to be capable of going that far with them and still have a punch left to throw.

Personally, I was fighting something of a lonely battle. I had come down from the high of being top scorer in the Leinster Final to the low of injury forcing me to sit and watch the semi-final. Now I was fit again for the final but circumstances had changed while I was out. Even when I came on as a sub against a very understrength Roscommon team in a challenge in Tullamore in the run-up to the final, I was ring-rusty and didn't do a whole lot to force the selectors into a fresh conclave.

Mooney picked up a slight thigh strain in training that week and didn't play in that game but I was around long enough to know that this was a precautionary measure and that his would be one of the first names down on the team-sheet for the final.

We had one final run out on the Saturday week before the Kerry game when Down played us in Tullamore. We were flying in that game — the last dress rehearsal before the real thing. Down were blown away by our fitness (which naturally was superior at that time of year), our power and our play. Their officials told us if we played like that again on the following Sunday week, we would be more than a match for Kerry.

Before the game I had a chat with Eugene over whether or not I should try to get some action. The consensus was that all we would be doing was tempting fate with the injury. Both of us knew that the team was already picked and my role would be, at best, that of a game-changing sub.

All the local papers gave us a very confident showing and while not screaming it from the rooftops declared that Offaly would win against Kerry.

Eugene used his own journalistic experience to accommodate reporters in the run-up to the final. In that era, news reporters usually would come down to Tullamore or Killarney or Tralee and report how colourful the places were and how the demand for tickets was driving prices through the roof. That sort of thing.

The managers would have an open session 10 days before the big match where the sporting press descended to get a few innocent quotes from players about how they felt the game would go.

McGee gave unprecedented access to his set-up. David Walsh, then of the Irish Press, was given permission to train for a night with us. Liam Kelly of the Sunday Independent was also brought inside the fold. It would result in him going against the grain on the national newspaper front by tipping Offaly to win in his paper.

I've never seen Eugene use so many provocative quotes to the media, basically inferring that Offaly's time had come. He said it so often that we began to believe him, just like Liam Kelly.

When it came to the mind games, the man was in a different league. It was only years later that even those of us in the group came to realise just how good he was.

I told him when I arrived at his house that I was so psyched up after the players' meeting that: "If a Kerryman stood in front of me now I'd go through the f**king wall to get him."

CHAPTER 18

AN EVE OF MATCH NIGHT CAP

It was nine o'clock on the Saturday night and I'd just come home from our final team meeting in Tullamore. I was still buzzing from the talk and just knew that if I stayed in I wouldn't sleep. My feet were itchy, I couldn't concentrate on what was on the television; I could hardly sit still.

Luckily, my brother-in-law Kevin Farrell had already been on to Veronne to see if I had arrived home yet. He told her he was feeling the need for a pint and wondered would I join him? She asked him if he had gone mad. "Sure if he was seen out tonight, he'd be shot," she joked.

Undeterred, Kevin rang back again and this time he got me. I repeated what Veronne had said but added truthfully: "Having said that, I could murder a drink right now — have you anything up there in your place?"

He said he had.

In his own book 'It's All News To Me', Kevin recalled that he asked me to pick up a bottle of lemonade to go with the bottle of brandy he had in his house. I went into McCormack's to get the provisions, and Kevin joked when I got to his place that the patrons must have been mightily impressed in the pub to see me buying a mineral and heading home for the night.

According to his book, seemingly I told him when I arrived at his house that I was so "psyched up" after the players' meeting that "if a Kerryman stood in front of me now I'd go through the f**king wall to get him." And in that deadpan humour of his, he added: "And that was before he got any brandy inside him."

At first the women made us measure the drinks by using a stainless steel egg cup but after a few, the cup fell on the ground and we poured straight from the bottle until we polished off the bottle.

I totally relaxed in this company where I could talk freely about the game. I told Kevin my big fear was if I was brought on just for the sake of it if Kerry were winning well or indeed in the unlikely scenario that Offaly were well ahead. I said that I'd nearly prefer not to get a run at all than to go through one of those meaningless cameos.

It was during that chat that it dawned on me that if I got called into the action, it would probably be late on when Offaly was behind. I wasn't sure I liked that scenario — the one I preferred in my own head would have been to get on early and play like I did in the Leinster Final

Then I got it in my head that I wanted to phone the late Fr John McWey, who was PP in Kilcock. He had been in Edenderry from 1951 to 1975 and is still a famous figure in the town. He was often seen pacing the canal bank praying, while in latter years and since his death, he was considered a lucky man, and as Kevin put it, "a man with a miraculous cure."

I spoke to him for a good little while and ended by explaining: "Now you know Father, that I'm only a sub tomorrow?"

"I know that Seamus, but you'll be brought in, and you'll score a goal. Goodnight now," he said.

After all that, I was ready to go home. I'd say I left Kevin and Eileen's house at about one in the morning. I had done my talking about the match, spoke to Fr. McWey so I knew for sure that I wouldn't spend the night tossing and turning.

It was psychological. I wanted to have a good night's sleep so that I would be ready to go if I was needed. That's the truth of it — plain and simple. I knew if I had stayed in and didn't do anything that I'd be awake half the night making up scenarios in my head — none of which would ever come to pass.

I went straight up to bed and was asleep before my head hit

the pillow. I slept like a baby and actually the drink relaxed me so much that I nearly slept it out the next morning.

I jumped out of the bed shortly before 10am and pulled up at Tommy Cullen's down the road to get petrol.

Tommy looked at his watch and said: "You're cutting it fine to catch the train in Tullamore at twenty to eleven."

I knew that only too well. I made tracks and luckily there was no traffic going that way. I got to the platform a few minutes before the train pulled in.

Once I boarded the train with the other players and the officials, you could sense the determination. In the carriage, there was this mixture of dread and sense of purpose that every player feels on a day like this.

Those hours leading up to a big match drag...and there is a feeling of loneliness even in a group like we are now. For sure, it is a great honour to be picked to represent your county but it is also a great responsibility. Players want to do well for their families and parishes but they are also very mindful that things can go wrong on the day and they can be responsible for losing a big game.

That was always a dread of mine and it happened in '76 in a Leinster championship match against Meath in Croke Park when I was captain. Now as I looked around me on our way with the intention as a group of bringing home Sam Maguire and depriving Kerry of the five-in-a-row, I could see even the most experienced players in the carriage were suffering bouts of nerves. From my own experience of a decade earlier, I knew they would continue to feel this way until they ran out onto the pitch and freed the butterflies on the green sward of Croke Park.

In many ways, younger players deal far better with these situations. For a start, they are more carefree and have their whole careers in front of them. While this Offaly team had a spine of experience, it also had plenty of youth on its side.

John Guinan was only 20 as was Padge Dunne — they were the babies of the team but two tough performers despite their age. Mick Lowry and Liam Currams were only a year older at 21, Matt, Brendy an Johnny were 23 year olds while Gerry Carroll and Tomás O'Connor were just 24.

In ascending order after that Richie was 27, Pat Fitzgerald was 28 and both Mick Fitz and Liam O'Connor were 29, Liam's birthday was the Monday before the final. That meant there were only two players who started against Kerry in their thirties — Furlong who was 36 and Seánie who was 30. When I came on I made it three old guys as I was just gone 31, while my brother Stephen was 27.

It gave an average starting age of just over 25 to the Offaly team as against 27 to Kerry, who had five players on the field at throw-in time who had turned 30.

Yet as the train careered into the outer suburbs of Dublin for a noon landing, I knew Offaly wouldn't lose out through inexperience. McGee had spent six long seasons with this team, adding a new player or two every year and losing one or two who were either too old or not of the temperament that he demanded, if first Dublin and then Kerry were to be overcome.

The full-forward line had a combined age of under 70, yet if fate had ordained it otherwise and allowed them play longer together, they could have formed one of the best inside lines of all time to compare with that of Sheehy, Liston and Egan from Kerry or later the O'Rourke, Stafford and Flynn inside trio from Meath.

All the while on that journey to Heuston Station, my mind kept flickering from the present where I was surrounded by Offaly players and mentors, to the future when I was creating images of coming on as a sub.

While I didn't have the constant worry that the starting players felt, inside I envied them the privilege of those nerves. It meant they would be on the pitch for the start of the game. I had to think beyond all that stuff because I knew it would mess with my head if I let it. I had to believe I would get the opportunity to make a contribution. In some ways I'd started that thinking process the previous night when talking to Kevin.

On the journey up to Croke Park, various things played on my mind — it occurred to me that it would be a hollow victory if after coming back, I picked up a medal but didn't see any final action at all as happened in 1971.

I banished that negative flow in my mind by plugging in to the positivity around me. I told myself that I wanted every player to do well for Offaly and if I was called on, early or late, then I'd do the very best I could.

McGee and the group of selectors he had around him had adopted a very positive approach from the moment we qualified for the final. Forget his play-acting about having no chance or not turning up on the day, he did all that to convince Kerry that they had no need to worry their heads about Offaly stopping them winning the five-in-a-row.

He had worked assiduously both individually and collectively to convince the players that they were good enough to win. When you consider the standing of that Kerry team — even then generally considered the greatest of all time — that took some doing. He dismissed how terribly we had performed in the semi-final as a good thing to get out of our system.

He convinced us that with our savage level of fitness, our detailed preparation and the game plan he had set out, we had it in us to match them stride for stride. He went so far as to tell us he expected us to be ahead at half-time, then Kerry would have their purple patch after the break and if we didn't let them put us away, we could catch them in the final furlong.

So all the work had been done, now it was down to those last two or three long hours that everyone was just wishing away so that the action could commence. The minutes leading up to a final go both slow and fast — there are times you feel that you are even thinking in slow motion. Every player is in a world of his own and will only switch back into the collective when someone starts talking.

You are entering the zone — the pre-match place where the past, present and future collide. It is indeed an unreal location.

All you can do is nod and give out strong body language; fist pump the lads you meet in the dressing room, encourage them with words that come out automatically.

"Horse into them."

"Leave nothing out there."

"From the word go..."

◆ ◆ ◆ ◆

We are in a cocoon now except I notice one thing — it has turned into a really shite day outside. The word is it will likely rain for much of the game. Still it is the same for both teams and the weather should never be used as an excuse.

The seconds, the minutes are now galloping by and McGee delivers his rallying speech to the troops. It has gone down well. Just as we are about to leave the dressing-room, Seánie Lowry calls us in and gives this incredibly poetic and spiritual observation about what an All-Ireland final means to ordinary people. He had been at his Uncle's wake two nights before across the border in Moate, Co Westmeath. While at the Edwards' house a man named Declan Carolan approached him and in conversation over the following 15 minutes, he put something in Lowry's head that he felt he should share with the rest of the team just before they left the dressing-room in Croke Park on Sunday afternoon.

Michael Foley recorded the moment for posterity in his excellent book on the Offaly-Kerry final called 'Kings of September'.

And then the moment came for Seánie to share the tale. "Remember lads, today you are playing for yourselves, your family and county but also for people you will never see, people you will never meet. You will have people all over the world, in America, in Australia, New Zealand who will have their chests out Monday morning if Offaly beat Kerry, but you will never see them or have the feeling they're feeling.

"There's two days people take off in a year — the Grand National and the All-Ireland football final. There are old women living down lonely roads in Donegal, Clare and Fermanagh and they're rooting for you today but you'll never meet them. You'll never realise the lift you'll give them if you beat Kerry today.

"You are carrying a great and noble tradition, generations of players from Walsh Island, Ferbane, Rhode, Edenderry and other Offaly clubs could never have imagined that an Offaly team could be so close to history. We cannot lose this game."

That was one powerful speech and when you look back on it, yes, it was about Offaly — pride in our players and the importance of winning for its people but it was also for people from other small counties who were living all around the world.

The next time I heard those words was at Eugene McGee's funeral in Longford Cathedral this year. The priest, Fr. Michael McGrath began his homily on May 9th by quoting Seánie's speech in its entirety out of the first chapter in Eugene's book.

As I understand it, there was no pre-plan for this extra gee-up to the players in 1982. It was a remarkable piece of judgment by Lowry that worked a treat for us on the day.

When he'd finished, the door was opened and we all burst out under the stand ready to fight tooth and nail — and with a greater belief than ever before that we could defy all the pre-match hype about Kerry and come back in as winners.

◆ ◆ ◆ ◆

The game turned out to be one of the best finals in history — a fascinating contest by two teams who were by some distance the best in the country at that time. Kerry, fast and skilful versus Offaly, fast and skilful. Kerry trying to make history by winning; Offaly trying to make history by preventing them from winning.

Kerry were unbackable because of what they had done previously; Offaly of course always embraced being underdogs... that position traditionally served us well.

Looking out from the shelter of the dugout, I liked the cut of our jib. You could see by the body language we were up for it and the way we started the game, it looked like the nerves were gone and if anything, Kerry were the ones showing signs that the occasion might be getting to them.

Everyone in the country knew what a talent Liam Currams was yet he hadn't really got going to the level we knew he could that year. In our final pep talk the previous night, McGee had extolled his virtues to the group, told him to use his assets such as positional sense and phenomenal pace to get possession but warned him not to kick the ball unless there was no alternative. Kicking wasn't his strong suit.

Currams nodded in quiet agreement at his manager's orders to pass the ball but it's a sign of the strength in his character that he set the tone for the rest of the lads on the pitch the following day. After the usual sparring between both teams, Liam drew first blood for Offaly when he sallied up the field on one of those unstoppable runs and kicked a glorious long-range point to open the scoring and raise Offaly hearts.

Kerry then hit a couple of points through Tom Spillane and John Egan before Pat Fitzgerald stormed up the pitch to emulate Currams' achievement by scoring on the run from the other side. It was tit-for-tat, Offaly going ahead, Kerry pegging us back and then when Bomber scored a point to make it 0-7 each after 26 minutes, I was aware that Eugene was shouting at me.

"Stephen Darby, get ready to go on," he said to me.

So, and this is genuine, Stephen and myself start taking off the tops of our tracksuits at the same time.

I'm thinking to myself: "McGee should make a better effort at remembering names. Poor Stephen is going to feel very let down when he realises it's me that he wants to go on."

Having watched the first 25 minutes of the game from close

quarters, I thought that our backs had done okay. It wasn't a case of anyone being taken to the cleaners, so I couldn't see where Stephen was to go. As we are both warming up all this is running through my head. Eugene looks straight at Stephen again and this time asks him: "Are you ready?"

Stephen's eyes are outside of his head as he puts on his gloves. He nods, McGee gives him a little push and he's gone out on the pitch to replace Mick Lowry. John Egan had started well and kicked a few points but I'm sure McGee factored in that the youngest Lowry member of the team was struggling with tight hamstrings and maybe reckoned that Stephen's no nonsense and sticky approach might curb the Kerry captain's influence better.

I had a little laugh to myself as I turned back into the dugout and put my top back on. I was thrilled to see Stephen going on and the fact that my brother was now playing in an All-Ireland final outweighed any personal disappointment I felt. Anyway, if the Offaly selectors were on their blow by making such an early substitution, I reasoned that they might have me on sooner than expected.

The team continued to put it up to Kerry and at one stage the other two Lowrys took over as Seánie became the third member of our half-back line to score while Brendy kicked two points in a row to give us a three point cushion. But two points, one from a Mikey Sheehy free and one from Jack O'Shea meant we were only leading by a point at the interval — Offaly 0-10; Kerry 0-9.

Once the second half started, I began to drift in and out of real time. I was watching the match, all the time preoccupied with how much was left on the clock and whether I would get the chance to get on?

Then Stephen was adjudged to foul Egan and I felt terrible when the penalty was awarded. I was out of my bubble again. I've looked at this incident and read about it again and again since and I think it was harsh enough to give the penalty. I don't think Stephen did a whole lot wrong. John Egan went down but got up and then Stephen put the squeeze on him again and maybe it was the fact that there was a second falling meant it was an easier decision for the referee to make.

Once it was given, there was nothing to do but accept it. It was slow motion time in my head once again... Mikey Sheehy's run up... Furlong's defiant save... the reaction of the crowd... and the relief and gratitude I felt that Stephen would not now be blamed if we lost.

Someone then shouted that there were about 20 minutes to go. That brought me back into the moment. I looked down to see if I could catch McGee's eye?

I couldn't.

He was up and down the line, totally caught up in every play of the game. There was nothing there to gladden a sub's heart — no selectors' huddle, no faces scanning the dugout, no shout of a name to get ready.

Despite missing the penalty, Kerry had gained a stranglehold on the game just as our manager had predicted. They would have gone four points in front if Sheehy had scored a goal from the penalty; instead the ball was cleared up the pitch and Mooney fired over a great score from Padge's pass to level matters for the ninth and final time.

Having been in charge of teams myself since then, I now realise that when a game is this close, it is hard to make changes. As predicted, the Kerry surge arrived as they took over in the middle third and went four points up thanks to two excellent scores from Seán Walsh, backed up by one each from Tom Spillane and Egan again.

They were now dominating like the old Kerry and if Jacko twice and Mikey hadn't been just off with their shooting, the holders would have gone six, maybe seven points up.

At this time, Offaly were struggling to cling onto Kerry's coat-tails and needed to do something before it was too late. The selectors brought out Richie and Gerry to midfield.

Straight away they made an impact which was helped by the fact that key Kerry players dropped back into defensive mode to protect the lead they had.

Finally, McGee scoured the subs' bench behind him and shouted at me to strip. I didn't know exactly what time was left but I knew there wasn't much. I was down beside him in an instant, ready to go on without any great warm up.

He told me to move in around the square and to get Brendy to move out a little but stay closer than they had been doing. I replaced John Guinan at right half forward who up to then was marked by Kerry's left half back, Tommy Doyle. When I went in, I picked up Tommy and then kept running until I got to Brendy. I gave him the sideline instructions as McGee had given them to me. That should have been a simple cop by the Kerry management team on the sideline... send Tommy back out with Brendy and leave Ger O'Keeffe, a specialist corner back, inside on me.

In fact, the Kerry selectors and Ger should have been delighted to see Lowry move away from goal because in addition to the three points he got, he had the ability to score a goal out of nothing.

I knew as I went in that if I got possession, there was only one option. The way the game had gone gave me no reason to change my mind.

Matt would say later that he was disappointed with his own performance but his head was working when others weren't that well tuned in. He clipped over a few frees to keep us in touch while Páidí got his second to score Kerry's last point. Seánie then 'engineered' a free and Matt pointed again, even though way up in the Hogan Stand, Mícheál O'Hehir was wondering if he would go for a goal.

That's the way it was set up then — two points between the teams with three minutes to go. I nearly got possession up my side but despite getting my hands on the ball twice, it was cleared up the field. The thought then crossed my mind that I mightn't get another chance. All I could do was hang in around the 13 metre line and hope that we'd manage to create something in the time left.

While part of me panicked that there might not be an opportunity, an echo deep inside the chambers of my mind whispered that all was not yet lost.

CHAPTER 19

ABOUT THAT GOAL — INSIDERS' VIEWS

I've already described my own memories and thoughts about that goal scored against Kerry. Since then, I've had the chance to go back on the video and listen to Mícheál O'Hehir's commentary which I think was the best he ever did. It was as if his intuition told him there would be late, late drama. To see how others involved felt, I've asked some people both on and around the team for their views as the clock ticked down on that Sunday afternoon, September 19.

'Nine minutes to go — Charlie (Nelligan) comes out to take the free...it's 0-15 to 0-12 in favour of Kerry, but they're not out of the woods yet...' (RTÉ Commentator, Mícheál O'Hehir)

Leo Grogan (Offaly Selector 1982) — I have a clear memory of what happened on the sideline before we made the substitution because I was involved with Eugene (McGee) and Paddy Fenlon in making it.

A few minutes before we sent Darby on, Eugene had turned to us and said: "We'll have to do something lads, the forwards are drifting out too far. Look there is no one staying in near the goal."

We decided that we would make a change. Paddy reminded us that at our eve of the match meeting we had agreed to bring Martin Fitzpatrick on first in the forward line simply because he was flying in training. We had talked the night before about Seamus and what he could do but we still had a concern over his fitness.

He was the leading scorer from play in Offaly club football that year. Paddy and I had initially approached Eugene in June and said: "We can't ignore what Darby has to offer" and his immediate response was: "Ok so, let's get him in."

It was a great move because Seamus was Man Of The Match in the Leinster Final where he scored 1-3 in the first half. Then he got injured and missed the semi-final against Galway and there was a doubt remaining over the hamstring for the final.

In the huddle on the sideline in Croke Park with Paddy and myself and despite what we had decided on the previous night, Eugene piped up: "What about Darby?"

I said: "I'd agree totally with that. He'll know what you mean about lying in around the goal and he'll get the other lads to stay in as well."

Paddy, Seán Foran and PJ Mahon (the other selectors) all nodded their approval.

Eugene then called Seamus and had a private few words with him that I didn't hear but I distinctly remember seeing him pointing towards the Railway End goal as if he was emphasising that Darby should go right in towards the Kerry goal.

Despite popular belief, there wasn't a 2-2 vote on the sideline with Eugene having the casting vote. The amazing thing about our group of selectors was that we never once put anything to a vote; we did everything by consensus.

Nor was there anyone from outside telling us what to do. I accept that Eugene Mulligan, who was at the far end of the dugout, may have shouted in our direction to bring on Seamus. There was so much noise coming from the stands that I certainly didn't hear him say that and Eugene has said previously that he didn't hear him either.

We did what we always did; we considered our options. Eugene put forward a player (Darby) and we made a judgement on the merits of the situation in which we found ourselves. We were happy to reverse our decision from the night before because now there was a different set of circumstances.

With only seven or so minutes left, the risk of Darby's injury recurring was much less a factor than if we had made a substitution in the forwards in the first half. And that's how we came to change our minds and he came to make history.

'Seamus Darby has come on now as John Guinan is fouled...he (Darby) is now taking a position, we will see who is going off... and John Guinan is going off as Matt Connor kicks it over the bar and the score is now 0-16 for Kerry and Offaly 0-13 with what, about six minutes to go...' (Mícheál O'Hehir)

John Guinan (Offaly forward) — After going off, I headed towards the dugout and because it was raining, I put on Seamus's tracksuit to keep me warm. Myself and Mick Lowry sat down together outside on the side line, just talking and watching the game.

Did we know there was a goal in Offaly? We didn't know for sure but we'd seen the forwards who were still out there, especially the likes of Seamus, Brendy, Matt and Johnny, score all kinds of goals in training and knew anything was possible.

Matt Connor (Offaly forward and free-taker) — To me, it was all about staying in the game... if we could keep the scoreboard ticking over, then there was always the chance that we might conjure up a goal.

Richie Connor (Offaly Captain) — I don't believe Seamus was brought in to play left corner forward because Brendy was the best corner forward in the country and he knew how to take a chance if it fell to him. I'd say it would be more accurate to say that Darby went on instead of John Guinan at half forward but was told to push in and stay close to goal. I think it just happened that he ended up in there one-on-one with Tommy Doyle. Mind you, I'm not complaining because, he's very skilful, he'd a reputation of knowing how to stick one away and it was no surprise to me that he delivered the goal when he got the ball.

'A free to Offaly and will Matt Connor be satisfied with the point? He is, he taps it over the bar? And now the score is 0-17 to 0-14 with less than four minutes left ...' (Micheál O'Hehir)

Matt Connor — Pointing the frees was just to keep us in the game. That mentality I suppose came from often winning late with Walsh Island back in Offaly or in Leinster club games. We had this thing of always trying to hang in there by doing the right thing to give the team the chance of winning. At the club, we'd often win a game in this fashion and that was all I was trying to do here.

Richie Connor — We were two points down... we had to hope that a chance would come along. We threw caution to the wind in those last six or seven minutes.

'And again I wonder is there a goal in the game somewhere? Time ticking away.....Charlie Nelligan with the kickout...'
(Micheál O'Hehir)

John Guinan — That was the thing McGee drilled into us — that we might need a goal. Every night in training he'd drive (Martin) Furlong mad by having Matt and the boys taking shots on him at the end of a session. Looking back now, it was marvellous foresight on his part to get us used to the idea that we just might need a goal.

'A line ball for Offaly and about three minutes left — three minutes, three points. Richie Connor to Liam Currams to Seán Lowry and the referee awards a free in to Offaly dead straight in front of the goal... on the 20 metre line and sure-ly Matt Connor will try, and I underline the word try, for a goal. Yes he is, he is standing back... no he's not, he taps it over the bar....two points between them. Just under three minutes left and is there still a goal left in the game?...'
(Micheál O'Hehir)

John Guinan — You could notice that Kerry weren't playing like Kerry. They never had a team coming at them like we did in those last 10 minutes and I suppose they didn't know what to do when they went behind because it was years since they found themselves in that position in Croke Park.

Stephen Darby — I was wedged to John Egan. We moved up under the Hogan Stand on the 50 yard line on the left hand side. He was talking; I said nothing, just tried my best to concentrate fully on marking him. He was such a danger. A minute or so before the goal he said to me when Kerry were in front by two points: "I think the ref's been a bit harsh on you lads today."

I think he must have thought Kerry had it won and maybe it was his way of mellowing the defeat for me. There were decisions going both ways but I think he felt they had it.

'There is a free to the Offalymen with two minutes left in the game. Kerry leading by two points. And it looks as if they are winning, the way the Offaly men are just diddling and dawdling there...' (Mícheál O'Hehir)

John Guinan — Eugene had kept telling us in training that we needed to be still close to them in the last 10 minutes — if we were, then we could pounce. We had gone through it so often that we didn't worry; it was as if we knew something would happen.

Richie Connor — When Seamus came in, it improved our chances of getting a goal. We already had lads there who could get you one — Matt, Brendy and Johnny.

'And here they come, this is Liam Connor, the full back. A high, lobbing, dropping ball, in towards the goalmouth. A shot — a goal, a goal, a goal for Offaly! There was a goal in the game. A goal, oh what a goal. And Offaly lead in the dying moments. Here it is again, the ball coming in...And the

ball is buried into the back of the net by the sub who came on, Seamus Darby and the score now is ... one point in it.... Sensation of sensations' ... (Micheál O'Hehir)

Stephen Darby — John (Egan) and myself were still down underneath the Hogan Stand. There was a cluster of players in front of me — Mick Fitzgerald was up there as well, and I didn't see who scored the goal. When I looked up again I could see Brendy celebrating with Seamus so I deduced it must have been Seamus who had scored it. But I didn't know for sure that he had.

Richie Connor — I knew it would take a moment of magic to win the game. I was one of the troopers and wouldn't have been capable of doing it but the lads inside were. It was Darby who provided the moment of magic for us in the end.

Matt Connor — I was waiting for the rebound (laughs)! It was a long ball, I was in around the goal but a bit to the right of the square. If it came in my side, I would have been on it. But it came in more across and I left it to Darby when I saw him going for it. He didn't need any help because he was as good a finisher as there was playing that time.

John Guinan — The goal was something else — all I remember is Mick and myself jumped up and bear-hugged each other. It was such a great feeling. Then shortly after the final whistle I saw my mother on the pitch and the two of us embraced. A stand-out memory to last a lifetime for sure.

Padge Dunne (Offaly midfielder) — I didn't even think of celebrating. I never went near Darby, I was close to him but I didn't have time to congratulate him or anything like that. I remember thinking that someone better get back quick so I sprinted as fast as I could towards our own goal and said to myself that we've got to defend now. I didn't know exactly what we had to defend but I felt it was best if we could stop them from scoring. I should have been looking for my own man but at that stage, I didn't even know where he was.

'Offaly taking a free on the far side... and they are in no hurry whatsoever...' (Micheál O'Hehir)

Richie Connor — I got terrified the second the goal went in. I knew we were a point up and I estimated there were two minutes or so left but I was absolutely terrified we'd blow the lead. We should have managed our possessions better when we got it from the kick out after the goal. Matt should have been allowed to take a free but he wasn't. He was capable of keeping the ball in Offaly hands and I was surprised he wasn't called over for that free. Then we were sloppy in possession and Kerry did get the chance I was dreading.

I was actually back there alongside Furlong when he came out along the end line and then tried to fist the ball. I thought he'd pop it to me and I feared the worst when Mikey Sheehy intercepted the hand pass to Stephen Darby and kicked it high in across our goal.

Padge Dunne — I don't have much memories of the game except for those last few minutes. And I wasn't thinking anything like... now we have scored the goal that is going to beat Kerry. My thoughts were — we still have a job to do. I remember Mick Fitzgerald was up right beside Seamus and he was totally switched on because he only focused on following Mikey Sheehy wherever he went. I can see him immediately after the snap of the goal staring into Sheehy's face. I said to myself... "If Mick is up here, who is minding the house?"

Stephen Darby — My mind clicked into a different zone. With the goal in the bag, I had to keep doubly close to John Egan if that was possible. I knew they would get down the field and try to equalise or score a goal and win it. I remember Furlong came out along the end line and his fist pass to me was intercepted. The ball went in from there to our square.

'It drops into the hands of the waiting Seán Lowry... the game is over... what a game... what a game...' (Micheál O'Hehir)

Padge Dunne — No one on the team knew how much time was left except Lowry. Jack (as we called him) knew because he had been there before on All-Irelands and he kept one eye on the big clock over the scoreboard.

After the goal, I burst a gut to track back and when Tom Spillane got on the ball I was about 30 yards away. I was praying "please don't pass it" because Bomber was on his own and screaming for the ball. Then when I got closer, I kinda thought: "You can pass it now if you want."

I went straight back into our square. Then I watched the ball coming in from Mikey Sheehy's delivery and I saw Lowry was under it with his eyes transfixed on the ball. I shouted to him: "You're all on your own, Jack".

About 20 years later, he asked me out of the blue one night if I remembered what I'd said to him before he got possession.

"Perfectly," I replied.

"Padge, they were the sweetest words I ever heard in an All-Ireland final," he said with a big smile on his face.

You see he had just glanced at the big clock, knew time was up and once he got the ball in his possession, he said he wasn't going to let it go until he heard the final whistle.

And that's how the game ended with Seánie charging out with the ball over his head in triumph.

Stephen Darby — When the whistle blew, I turned to John (Egan) and could see he was shell-shocked. He was captain of their team that had just lost an All-Ireland in the most dramatic circumstances. We shook hands but he couldn't say a word. I remember thinking how cruel sport was — here I was overjoyed and the man beside me was totally devastated as the pair of us lived through the same moment.

I didn't get to meet Seamus after the game until we got to the steps of the Hogan Stand. He'd been hoisted up on shoulders with people carrying him this way and that; that wasn't such a problem for me. We embraced there and it was a special moment — one for the ages.

CHAPTER 20

ABOUT THAT GOAL — 37 YEARS AFTER THE EVENT

Richie Connor — From a personal point of view, and I'd say all the other lads would feel the same, the goal didn't change us in terms of how we lived. It made all of us All-Ireland winners — and it was a special All-Ireland when you consider Kerry were on the cusp of history and we deprived them of it.

It makes you proud when you meet other players who recognise you as an All-Ireland winner. If we had lost that game, we wouldn't have that status. It elevated everything. That is the main thing about getting over the line as we did against Kerry, we are part of that elite group who have won All-Irelands.

If that goal had not arrived and Kerry had won, we would only have got one or two All Stars. Instead we got seven — Furlong, Liam O'Connor, Mick Fitzgerald, Seán Lowry, Liam Currams, Padge Dunne and Matt.

Furlong won the Man Of The Match and Player Of The Year and I ended up winning the Offaly Player of the Year from the Offaly Express that year. So to sum up, the goal changed things like that for us all, and we are truly grateful for that.

Padge Dunne — It is probably one of the most important things that has happened to me outside of getting married and having kids.

It was a huge day in the history of Gaelic football but it's only as the years slip by that you fully appreciate that. Certainly, I didn't have any great understanding of what we had done in the immediate aftermath. It has travelled down the years like few other moments in the GAA and we, who were lucky enough to be there, have travelled along with it.

John Guinan — Padge (Dunne) and myself were both only 20 at the time but here we were All-Ireland winners at such a young age.

It was a huge boost to my confidence. It was great for my family, my club and of course the county. That was in the shorter term.

Looking back, it helped me to become a leader in the club, because to play football as an All-Ireland medal holder was a great honour and I knew that. I often thought the opposite down the years — what would have happened if Darby didn't get that goal? I know I'd have dreaded going back into training, enduring those winter nights in Rhode and no guarantees the following year.

If I was to put it in a nutshell about that goal, I'd say it made me feel a foot taller — actually, it made all of us a foot taller then — and I think it still makes us feel that way to this day.

Matt Connor — It was huge for us to get across the line and win an All-Ireland and we all have to be thankful that we got our medals in '82 from that goal. There is no doubt though that in beating Kerry the hunger left us. Yes, we were competitive for a year or two afterwards but we weren't driven like we were before that final. If we hadn't won that year, I'd like to think we would have kept going until we did win one, but there were no guarantees.

What amazes me most about the goal is that people still want to talk about it — it is truly a moment in time.

CHAPTER 21
AFTER THE BALL WAS OVER

The week following on from the Kerry match in 1982 was one of the maddest I ever experienced in my life. The Sunday night was one long adrenalin rush not just for me — but for the players and all those associated with the team. We went from Croke Park to the reception and then we headed for the Ambassador Hotel in Kildare where we were booked in to stay.

Not many players saw much of bed that night. One of my abiding memories was of myself and Johnny Flaherty, who scored the winning goal for the hurlers the previous year against Galway in the All-Ireland final, being both bumped up so high by the crowd that we were actually hitting the ceiling. Everyone was on a high and it was near six o'clock in the morning before I got close to my bed.

The following day the two counties met up for lunch in the Burlington Hotel and it was then that for the first time I began to look at the All-Ireland from Tommy Doyle's corner and I was sad to think that someone always pays for someone else's glory.

The Offaly factor clicked in again as we made our way by train from Heuston Station in Dublin down to Tullamore where half the county seemed to have turned out to welcome us. As we were pulling into the station, I saw one banner 'Furlong Rhode A Darby Winner' which has stayed with me down through the years. We inched down High St to O'Connor Square and finally made it across to the Bridge House. What a night of revelry and I remember it was another six o'clock in the morning occasion as myself and a few others headed for Edenderry.

I slept for a few hours and got up at around 11am. The celebrations were in full swing when I put my head inside McCormack's pub situated right beside where I had my shop. It was jammed with supporters and Paddy gave me a huge hug before pouring a full bottle of champagne over my head.

I was reeking of drink and was trying to dry myself with a towel when word came that RTE had rung next door and wanted to know if I would become one of the participants on the Superstars programme.

Many people my own age or somewhat younger would know immediately what that programme was but for younger readers, it was a competition presented by the late Jimmy Magee which got people from different sports to compete against each other. The aim was to find an 'Irish Superstar' and the winner would then compete against the winners in all other countries who entered the competition.

It was very popular in its day and I think Pat Spillane and Bernard Brogan senior were two of our top exponents in the event.

When they asked me to do it, it was hard to turn down despite suffering from the affects of too much revelry.

I rang them back and said I would.

"When is it on?" I asked, thinking it might be a few weeks away.

"Tomorrow," came the reply.

Gerry Carroll was in my company when the call came through and he made sure I accompanied him as he already had been invited to take part. I was filling in for Mikey Sheehy who had pulled out the previous day. It was all a bit mad but I went with the flow. Gerry and I were told to book into the Royal Marine in Dún Laoghaire the following evening and to be ready for an early start to competition on the Thursday.

I left McCormack's and headed out to visit my mother and father. It was the first time I'd seen them since before the match and I wanted to share an hour with them. It was a precious time and I could see how proud they were. Mammy made tea for Veronne and myself. That visit was for the ages and I still remember every moment vividly. I then dropped Veronne back into Edenderry and picked up Gerry again. We decided we'd head for Dublin but would call into the Woof Mooney's on our way. The minute he saw us, he threw up a litre of Hennessy's brandy. The place was hopping; everyone was on a high. The feeling was it wasn't everyday that Offaly would be the centre of such GAA history. I could have stayed there all night the craic was so good. However, it was now late and we decided we'd go back to Edenderry and get a friend to drive us to Dublin. That way we could spend another hour in Edenderry, swing across to Tullamore where most of the team were and then head much later than planned to Dun Laoghaire.

We were supposed to check in at nine o'clock but it was two in the morning before we got there. We'd phoned ahead from Tullamore and two of the other competitors, Wexford hurler, George O'Connor and Kilkenny's Christy Heffernan said they'd have two pints waiting for us. Fair play to the lads for staying up to congratulate us on our win. We had those pints and a few more before we hit the bed.

What a way to prepare for some serious sporting competition only hours away. Luckily, the organisation wasn't anything like it would be nowadays because no one seemed to pass any remarks although myself and Carroll looked like something the cat had dragged in.

The organisers had bigger problems to solve when we arrived. Christy was a size 14 in shoes and they couldn't find a pair of runners or spikes big enough to fit him. He had no choice but to run in his boots which he had brought along with him.

And so to the action. Here's a quiz question for you — in a race involving George O'Connor, Neil Cusack, Noel Skehan and myself over 100 metres, who would you say won it?

Believe it or not I did. I wouldn't have had a reputation for being a runner but I was always good at the sprint distances. That was one of the major reasons I enjoyed training. Like everyone else, I hated the endless laps that were part of every session in those times, but I revelled in short, sharp races.

I'd say I surprised the boys as well because George was another Currams the way he covered the ground while Neil Cusack was an international athlete.

I had a fair amount of practice that summer sprinting with some top class performers. One of the memories is the countless races Matt, Gerry, Liam and myself had down the full length of the pitch in Ballycommon.

Those three were known speedsters but the four of us regularly breasted the tape together. At 31, it gave me a great lift just to be able to stay close to those greyhounds.

After the first event in Belfield, Mick Dunne arrived from nearby RTE. He'd heard on the grapevine that I was taking part and wanted to interview me. He had already done it on the Sunday after the game but taking part in the 'Superstars' had given the All-Ireland story extra legs.

After winning the sprint, the next competition was on the bicycles. I loved cycling but I had seldom if ever been on one of these racing bikes with the ultra thin wheels. I was terrified and could hardly maintain my balance on the very tight tartan track at UCD. The achievement was the fact that I finished that race in one piece rather than being competitive.

Shortly afterwards, I did one other event and then hit the proverbial wall. The week's drinking caught up with me and I was totally exhausted and couldn't move a muscle. I had no choice but to pull out of the rest of the competition. Gerry stayed in and did very well. He won his sprint and was very competitive without actually winning the overall title.

For me it was time to relax after the hectic weekend. I needed to get away from all the madness. I was sure if I put my head down and went missing, all the hype would go away.

The following Saturday week, Veronne delivered our third and youngest child, Shay in St Vincent's Hospital, Dublin.

The photographers came to the hospital and there was a

picture of the two of us and Shay across the Sunday Independent and other news outlets the following day. I was pretty sure then that this would be the end of all the publicity. Instead, it was only the beginning.

*He took the criticism on board
and also took the humiliation
of having four strong-willed
new selectors foisted on him
by the county board.*

CHAPTER 22
1983 — THE LEINSTER FINAL AMBUSH

Eugene McGee didn't look for scapegoats when things went wrong — he took his reverses on the chin. He learnt a big lesson from the 1979 Leinster Final and without it, we mightn't have won an All-Ireland with that Offaly team. He shipped a lot of heavy criticism from within the county after that game for not making moves to maximise the numerical advantage we had against Dublin. That was the match where Jimmy Keaveney was sent off following an altercation with Ollie Minnock in the second half.

We all can be very wise after the event but in the cold light of day leaving Liam O'Connor as the extra man on the edge of our own square when Dublin were lording it at midfield wasn't the smartest thing to do. Neither he nor his selectors of that time covered themselves in glory that day.

He took the criticism on board and also took the humiliation of having four strong-willed new selectors foisted on him by the county board. It was a clear message — not from the top table where both John Dowling and Fr. Heaney still offered strong support — but from the delegates that they had lost confidence in him as a manager.

These new lads, Mick O'Rourke, Noel Magee, Martin Furlong and Johnny Cooney were nobody's 'yes' men and that winter and into the spring, they, in effect, took control. There was often the sight of McGee having to go to them cap in hand seeking to make changes during games.

He referred at length to this episode in his own book 'The GAA In My Time' and recalled how he decided before a prestige tournament match played in Ferbane against Galway to outflank the others. He did so by presenting them with the team he had picked by himself. The selectors, quite understandably, took umbrage and went to the other side of the pitch. Offaly won the match and that night, the four offered their resignations. They were accepted immediately by Fr. Heaney, who sent each a short note to thank them for their services.

Then the Co Chairman (Fr. Heaney), the County Secretary (John Dowling) and the Assistant Secretary (Br Sylvester Carney) were co-opted to act as interim selectors before another quartet with strong Offaly backgrounds were appointed. These men would be easier to work with but were more tuned in to McGee and how a management team should operate as a united group. They were PJ Mahon (Walsh Island), Paddy Fenlon (Edenderry), Leo Grogan (Ferbane) and Seán Foran (Edenderry).

By engineering the resignations of the previous selectors and getting in older and more complementary personnel into his backroom team, McGee made himself a stronger and more independent operator on the sideline from there until his decision to leave Offaly in '84.

After organising the coup, he faced a massive test of his calibre within a short period of time in the 1980 Leinster Final. Offaly failed to turn up in the first half and he went to town changing the team around at half-time. That in turn led to a much better second-half performance that brought a significant win for the county and himself. It was the first inter-county Leinster senior title on his watch. It was also the first defeat of Dublin in the province during the Heffo/Hanahoe era dating back to 1974.

If Eugene was still with us, the one thing I'd like to talk more to him about was what happened in 1983. He didn't hide behind excuses when saying: "I take personal blame for that defeat. We were too complacent. We thought we couldn't lose the match," he told Pat Nolan for his book, 'The Furlongs.'

That day it wasn't just him — players and supporters also had a cavalier approach in the run up to the final against Dublin. We didn't know that Heffo was on a mission after overhearing a derogatory remark from one of our players about how poor his team had been in the '82 Leinster Final. We also didn't realise that the hunger that drove us in '82 had been sated more than we imagined in the aftermath of that famous Kerry victory. Nor did we know that when it was put up to us by the Dubs from the start in '83, that we hadn't got it in us to come back and win.

That year is a 'what might have been' story in the history of this Offaly team. I think we were good enough to win back-to-back titles like the lads in '71-'72 but we took our eye off the ball. Maybe that is understandable in the context of how hard that squad had to fight to win one All-Ireland — beaten by Wexford in the Leinster quarter-final in '77, beaten by Dublin in the Leinster semi-final in '78, beaten by Dublin in the Leinster final in '79, beaten by Kerry in the All-Ireland semi-final in 1980 and then beaten by Kerry in the All-Ireland final in 1981 before finally beating Kerry and winning the All-Ireland final in 1982.

There were a lot of hills to climb in that journey for one ultimate success. And even though overall it was a young team, it had high mileage on the clock.

We didn't help ourselves in the build up to the final. We had a meeting in Larkin's pub in Edenderry the night before the game and no one foresaw any great problems. I remember Eugene said that we had beaten these lads by nine points the previous year and there was no reason why we couldn't do the same the following day and move on.

Without realising it, we were sitting ducks and Heffo was about to spring a classic ambush. The throwaway remark — something as innocent as "I thought they'd give us a better game of it" — was used by the Dublin manager to wind up his players.

He had sworn to a member of the Dubs backroom team

beside him on the day the remark was made that he'd search high and low around Dublin to find new players who would beat us the following year.

And he was as true as his word. The game was over by the end of the first half as Dublin tactically won the battle with their player placement and scored two killer goals in the run-up to half-time.

It is also worth remembering the context in which this Leinster Final was played. It came the week after Cork had beaten Kerry in the Munster final. I think our heads were in the wrong place as we felt that there was a different dynamic in place after Kerry were gone. We were thinking ...wasn't it great that they wouldn't be on the horizon after Dublin? That's what happened; we forgot to jump the fence in front of us. We were all to blame because we should have known better.

That was a good Cork team with Dinny Allen, Dave Barry and Jimmy Kerrigan. I'm not so sure how we would have fared against them in Croke Park anyway but the feeling was it would have been a lot easier with the Kerry lads out of the way.

Cork played Dublin off the park for most of the All-Ireland semi-final and Barney Rock got a late goal to force a replay. Dublin then travelled to Páirc Uí Chaoimh and annihilated Cork in their own backyard. It was arguably the best performance from the Dublin team of that time.

Had we beaten them in the Leinster Final, it would have been a 50-50 battle against Cork and Galway and ourselves in the final could also have gone either way. If we had prepared as well as the previous year, we could have won it, but it was no way nearly as clear-cut as the opportunity we had 10 years earlier to win three-in-a-row.

I am convinced to this day that 1973 was the one that got away. There was no surprise — it boiled down to the fact that Galway were fresher and we struggled to keep pace with them. We eventually lost by only two points, 0-16 to 2-8. I was hoping to get in for a run as a substitute but suffered from my own enthusiasm to impress earlier in the year. It was a lesson that I never forgot. We were travelling down for a league match in Salthill and it was a real filthy day. I had been in bed all week with the flu. I remember Fr. Gilhooley asking me if I was alright to play and I said I was.

Actually I was so weak I was hardly able to tie my bootlaces. I never got a kick. The first ball I went for Joe Waldron hit me a belt and I didn't know which end of me was up after that. My reason for playing was that I figured if Murt (Connor) got in and did well, he would have an advantage over me for the corner forward spot the two of us were in competition for. In the heel of the hunt, neither of us got the position as Hughie Healy was picked ahead of both of us.

I suppose if I had been surer of my place, I would have told Fr. Gilhooley that I was not up to it. McTague or Cooney would have been up front, knowing they were automatic choices. I paid a big price because after that poor showing, I didn't get a minute on the pitch for the rest of that year.

In '83, any thoughts people had of back-to-back All-Ireland wins were gone long before the game was over. John Caffrey, who was a big fella, went in on Charlie Conroy in the corner but once the game started, pulled Charlie out around the middle and cleaned up. He was everywhere and put a nail in our coffin by volleying a goal just before half-time. That put Dublin 2-5 to 0-7 in front. Psychologically, it gave them more than a four-point lead as they headed into the dressing room.

Heffo's search between the '82 Leinster final defeat and the following year's campaign also unearthed Joe McNally, a 19-year-old burly figure who had been in goal for the Dublin minors in '82. He turned Joe into a really effective corner forward who scored 1-2 against us on top of causing our defence all sorts of trouble.

As players, we had become cocky and complacent and deserved what we got — a right hammering. In the end the Dubs won by five points 2-13 to 1-11 but if they had taken half their chances — Furlong saved a penalty on this occasion too from Brian Mullins — it could have been a much heavier defeat.

We were always playing catch-up and our sheer doggedness got it back to a three-point game after Matt Connor deftly finished past John O'Leary to momentarily raise our hopes. Barney Rock stuck over a free and McNally capped a great performance with his side's last score to put the issue beyond doubt and give Dublin a deserved win.

It's only fair to say that notwithstanding all the complacency, nothing worked for us at all on that day. Our two go-to forwards had serious off-days at the same time and that had seldom if ever happened before. Matt even missed a penalty that could have revitalised us. And of all people Brendy Lowry, who I'd never seen waste a chance for Ferbane or Offaly, missed an open goal.

I didn't play at all that day; I watched every minute as an unused substitute. Martin Fitzpatrick, the young lad who joined the panel the same day as me in '82, came on and did well, scoring a point. Charlie was the only change from the team that lined out in the All-Ireland final against Kerry the previous year. He came in for Mick Lowry in the full-back line but was later replaced by the same Lowry. Aidan O'Halloran also got a run and had a hand in the Offaly goal after replacing Gerry Carroll in the second half. These were all correct decisions because the way I felt, they deserved to get in ahead of me; the reality was that I hadn't much to offer.

In his book, Eugene lamented the fact that he didn't know anything about the throwaway remark that riled Heffo. If he had, he said he would have approached the match much differently. He would have had us ready for that ambush. As it transpired, this match effectively was the last hurrah of that Offaly team when it shouldn't have been.

"Unfortunately for me, I never heard about that comment until 24 years later when Offaly had a reunion. Had I been aware of it, I would have known that Heffernan was going to go to any lengths to teach that player a lesson, and also to teach Offaly and McGee a lesson. I would have prepared for a Heffernan onslaught," he explained.

Even when he was first told about it, Eugene was disinclined to believe such an incident had occurred. When it was confirmed to be the case, it made perfect sense to him because of the way Dublin were so wound up on that day.

I was 32 that year and had been out and about all winter and spring presenting trophies to youngsters and attending dinner dances for clubs up and down the country.

How could my head be in the right place? Yes, I was training but I was going through the motions more than chomping at the bit to get at Dublin again. The build up between '82 and '83 couldn't have been more different. Talking to most of the players since, they too would confirm that we had sleep-walked into that Leinster Final ambush.

It's the first time I've admitted this but one of the biggest mistakes I ever made football-wise was not retiring from inter-county football straight after the All-Ireland in 1982.

It's easy to see that now.

How could I ever replicate or emulate what had happened against Kerry? Without realising it, by going on, all I was doing was setting myself up for failure. I never was quite as interested in football again? I'd say if Rhode had gone out of the championship that year, I might have gone too. I was club captain and my one remaining ambition — a burning one at that — was to captain Rhode to an Offaly title. I'd have loved to do that for myself but even more so for my father, who was the proudest Rhode man I ever met.

It was great to win senior county medals in '67, '69 and '75 but it still burns a hole in me that I never got to lift the Dowling Cup as captain.

It took everything we had as a unit to stay with them and get out of their home patch still alive in the championship.

CHAPTER 23
MY LAST HURRAH

As I look back on the year 1984, I'm wondering was I mad to be even around at that stage? I certainly did no stock take to see what was left inside. Quite simply I carried on like before. In retrospect I probably didn't want to confront the fact that the Offaly journey was nearing an end.

In the Leinster championship, I came on as a sub against Longford in Pearse Park when we got the fright of our lives and were lucky to escape with a draw. Nine minutes into the second half, Longford led by 0-12 to 0-4 and everywhere you looked, Offaly were chasing shadows.

Our fullback line was up a stick and we were cleaned out at midfield as well. There seemed to be an ironic twist unravelling for Eugene where his own county would spell the end for him in Offaly.

I came on with about 20 minutes left as part of a number of positional changes. Johnny Mooney was switched out to midfield and once we got a few bits of possession through him, the Offaly sap began to rise. Before he moved, Mooney had fastened onto a great Richie Connor pass to bury the ball in the net.

We still had a big fight on our hands as Longford, with Dessie Barry and Mickey O'Hara playing like All-Stars, looked likely to score every time the ball went into their full-forward line. It took everything we had as a unit to stay with them and get out of their home patch still alive in the championship. I was in decent shape when I got the run and tried my hardest to win every ball and get it into our own full-forward line.

We beat them in Croke Park in the replay. That was the famous occasion where Furlong was unable to play and Offaly only had one goalie left in the panel — Dinny Wynne of St Rynaghs. McGee was outside the dressing room during the minor match and was told that Laz Molloy had just paid in and was definitely in Croke Park. There was a call for him to report to the Offaly dressing room put across the tannoy by the announcer. Laz answered it immediately and had time to go back to his car parked outside in one of the adjoining streets to retrieve his playing gear that luckily he had brought with him in the boot.

In the game, Longford hit the ground running again and had Offaly in all sorts of trouble after scoring a couple of first half goals.

Offaly brought Laz and myself on for the second half and he had a blinder in goal. I did well enough, scoring two points as we progressed to another Leinster semi-final against Dublin on a score-line of 3-15 to 3-10. Matt scored 2-5, the goals from penalties and Brendy scored 1-4.

The Co Board was then caught in a bit of a bind. Having agreed to bring forward the Dublin semi-final game by a week to facilitate a Neil Diamond Croke Park concert, they now found themselves minus seven players, including Liam Currams, who had knee problems.

Eugene wrote in the Sunday Tribune the following week — the morning of the semi-final — that if this was to be the last of his Offaly team, then it might be that Dublin — and Neil Diamond — were the twin architects of their demise.

Yes, we had injuries and several players lined out nowhere near 100 per cent fit. Despite that, there was no excuse for how badly we played. If September 19, 1982 had been a high watermark for Offaly football against Kerry, then the Leinster semi-final encounter against Dublin on June 24, 1984 was the bottom of the barrel. We were beaten by 0-13 to 0-5 and the fact that we got only one point in the second half accurately reflects how poor the forward division was that day.

After sitting out the previous year, I started this game alongside 12 of the Offaly side which had lined-out against Kerry in '82. Seánie Lowry had moved on to Mayo by then and Liam Currams and John Guinan were the other guys not on the team sheet with Aidan O'Halloran and Aidan Scally starting instead.

Matt Connor scored three points with Johnny Mooney, our best player, and Brendy Lowry, (sent off early in the second half), getting a point each. My own performance can probably be best summed up in the words of the local reporter who wrote: "Not until Peter Brady replaced Seamus Darby did Offaly promise anything in attack and even then it was a promise that remained unfulfilled."

Talk about an ignominious exit. That was my last game as an inter-county player and a poor one to end on for sure. It also brought an end to McGee's long association at the helm of Offaly football.

Unlike Kerry and Dublin, two teams who had come quickly out of nowhere to wins All-Irelands, it had taken Offaly six season to get over the line and win one. The Irish Independent's Liam Kelly was on the money in his Monday report when he stated: "Offaly had enough fit players to make a game of it but in the stealthy manner in which he brought about the decline of Dublin 1974-'79 and Kerry 1978-'82, old Father Time finally caught up with this Offaly squad".

I should have read the signs and been gone at that stage. I was at a funeral the day before and hadn't any expectation of playing at all. Due to the number of injuries, I was chosen at left-half forward, marking Pat Canavan. If I was picked in the corner, I might have had a chance but I didn't get a kick against Pat and Peter Brady came on for me at half-time.

Old Father Time indeed had the final say. I bowed out of inter-county that day with no fanfare and a sense of sadness that I had come to the end of the line. It was only then that I realised the extent of what I had missed between the age of 26-31 when I was in my playing prime but wasn't part of the Offaly squad.

*In Furlong's case, he should
be judged by the saves he
never had to make because
he was out like a light to
prevent a shot ever being taken.*

CHAPTER 24
A SALUTE TO FAITHFUL SOLDIERS '82

As I mentioned in an earlier chapter, I will be forever in debt to every one of the Offaly squad for the kindness they showed and the welcome they gave me when I was brought in from the cold in mid-'82.

There are some who I have become very close friends with since that time while to those I don't see that often, I still have fond memories from the training sessions and matches from that joyous time in our sporting lives. This is how I see them as I look back on that troop who soldiered together to win the county's last senior football All-Ireland.

Martin Furlong — Was there ever a nicer person off the field of play who was such a fierce competitor on it? Martin, the grand old man of that squad at 36, was a thorough gentleman, kind, soft-spoken and self-deprecating in civvies. When he pulled the Offaly or Tullamore jersey on, he'd go through the proverbial brick wall to get to a ball first. Some goalkeepers are judged — and rightly so — for the saves they make in a career. In Furlong's case, he should be judged by the saves he never had to make because he was out like a light to prevent a shot ever being taken.

The incident in the Leinster Championship last June (2018) between Dublin's goalkeeper, Stephen Cluxton and Longford forward, James McGivney in Croke Park reminded me of Furlong. I think the Irish Times at the time said that McGivney, who got sent off, had "poleaxed Cluxton in mid-air" after the keeper advanced from his goal to clear a high ball.

I could visualise Martin racing off his line, his tongue outside his mouth in total concentration and I can tell you the only one being poleaxed in such a scenario would have been the forward. Furlong wasn't a big man but he was all knees and elbows, as Stephen my brother can attest, and he packed an awful lot more into his hits than any other player I've ever seen play Gaelic football.

That Cluxton incident also reminded me of a club game I saw in O'Connor Park when a forward scored a goal against him. Later in company, the scorer told the guy who had passed him the ball never to do that again when playing Tullamore.

"Didn't you score?" said the other fella back to him.

"Yea, but that's only because Furlong slipped and even then he nearly killed me with a belt."

Actually Martin played a lot of his club football outfield, often at centre-forward or full-forward, and invariably he would have an influence on a game by bringing that same raw physicality to proceedings. He won a lot of possession for his team because he only saw the ball and then he could be relied on to give a simple pass to a better placed colleague. Tullamore won a championship in '77 playing off him in a year when they achieved the treble — minor, U-21 and senior championships.

Furlong was one of Offaly's golden generation along with Willie Bryan, Tony McTague and Eugene Mulligan. They won the minor All-Ireland in '64 and then were present when Offaly made the breakthrough in senior in '71 and '72.

Martin was the only one of that group still present in '82 when we beat Kerry where he was voted Man Of The Match and was later named Footballer of the Year.

People can talk all they like about my goal but the reality is that without Furlong making the penalty save from Mikey Sheehy, Kerry would have been gone over the hill and far away from whatever Offaly comeback was mounted.

His save changed that but even after we scored the goal, Kerry got up to our end of the park and could have forced a reply. Furlong again ensured that didn't happen and one of the last memories of that game is seeing him shuffle out along the end line fighting for the ball and doing all in his power to keep it away from Kerry hands.

Furlong fought for every inch in a game and it is fitting that he is up there on a pedestal as the only footballer in the county with four All-Ireland medals (one minor) in his vast trophy collection.

Mick Lowry — I marked him a good bit in training and in club matches. He was a tough, strong guy who I never looked forward to playing against. He didn't mind what way you wanted to play it — he could do it any way.

Mick was taken off in the final for my brother Stephen to come on. Now what people wouldn't know is that Mick had terrible trouble the whole summer with his hamstrings. I think Eugene McGee saw early on in the final that he wasn't able to stride out fully — and against John Egan you needed to be in the whole of your health. While Egan was on fire early on, I think it was the fact that Mick wasn't totally fit on the day that led to his being taken off in the first half. Certainly it wasn't lack of football because this lad could play, could mark and made sure any forward he was on earned their corn.

Liam O'Connor — The funny thing with Liam and myself is that I got to know him a lot better when we stopped playing than during the time we togged out together as Offaly teammates.

Yes, we'd always chat in and around the dressing room or if we bumped into each other at a club match but I couldn't honestly say I was friends with him around the time we won in '82.

The first time I really got to know him was a few years later after we had both retired from the county and I was in Dublin as part of my job as a salesman on the road.

I was up getting supplies one day and decided to go for a sandwich before making an afternoon of calls around the city. As I was going into the Harp Bar, I bumped into Liam and we agreed to meet up after work again that evening. In such situations where you have time to reminisce, I find that you can get to know a lad very well over a few pints.

After that night we became much closer. Liam had never taken a drink in his playing days and that showed his dedication as a player. He would come in to training, work hard to improve his fitness and his playing skills with the drills and then was gone home.

He didn't mix the same as say his first cousin Richie did. In fact Richie, who was only a month younger than Liam, used to tell us how his mother would complain: "Why can't you be more like Liam and come home early instead of staying out half the night?"

In later life Liam lived in Dublin and then moved to Waterford and with me living in London and other parts, it became harder to meet up. There were a few occasions at Offaly get-togethers where our friendship blossomed. News of his illness and then of his death rocked us all — he was the first of our panel to die and what made it all the harder to take was that he was a fit man and still only in his late fifties.

I spoke very little to Liam about the goal. He'd have a laugh now and then by saying he meant it as a pass to me. McGee had always emphasised the importance of accurate and long kick-passing and I know he was certain that Liam's 50 yard foot pass came from such practice. Regardless of how it came to be, it certainly worked for us on the day and as Eugene often wrote, you'd rarely see such a pass in the modern game.

Liam was very dedicated to making himself a better footballer as he didn't really make the breakthrough at under age level and forced himself into becoming a late developer through his commitment.

There was a time where he used to be a bit of soft touch in club games but once he got into the Offaly set-up, he learnt the dark arts of dragging you back without being seen and rooting the ball away from the danger area. Overall, he got much harder to play against. I never played against him directly in the local championship but when they started to use me as a full-forward after I'd gone back in 1982, every night I had to go toe-to-toe with him. By then, he was big, strong, quick and improved me just by the fact that I knew I had to be at my best to win some ball off him.

I maintain that Offaly had two factors — of course they had many more — but they had two that were unique in Gaelic football when playing that all-conquering Kerry side.

We had Liam, who was one of the only players that could handle The Bomber in the country — and we had Matt, who terrified every defence, even one as good as Kerry's. We knew from the time he scored 2-9 against them in the All-Ireland semi-final of 1980, that any day you had Matt Connor in your side, you wouldn't be too far away at the final whistle.

He is the one who made my goal possible because even when the ball was coming in from Liam, there were two or three top class Kerry players keeping their eyes on Matt more than me. And his presence gave me a better chance of scoring. If you look at a still from the time the ball is about to land, there is only Tommy and me on one side, while Matt and Johnno and Paudie Lynch and Jacko were all around him in front of the Kerry goal around the 13 metre line.

That is why when I think about the goal I am forever grateful to those two players, Liam and Matt, for the roles, one active, one passive, they played in making it happen.

In Matt's case there was another context as to why I think of him when that goal is mentioned. He had the wit to see when we were four points down that there was time to win the game if we kept chipping at their lead. So when we got the frees — one or two very soft in my opinion — and unlike Mícheál O'Hehir's commentary where he felt sure he would go for a goal, Matt kept us in a position to win the game.

I mean what would it have mattered if we had a free taker who had a rush of blood to the head and went once or twice for a goal. We'd still have been maybe four points down and a goal wouldn't have been enough. We'd probably have lost. And not too many would have the memory of my goal the way it is still there in the public consciousness half a lifetime after it happened.

Liam's outstanding defending is never mentioned in the context of that final either. If you watch the game back on video, you will see how his speed got him into a situation where he could use his strength and size to clear a very threatening Kerry attack in front of Furlong's goal. There is no doubt that he was one of those players who grew in stature in the surrounds of a big Croke Park game.

Mick Fitzgerald — Every team needs a Mick, a silent operator who gets the job done. If you told him: "Mick you're on Mikey Sheehy," Mick would nod and go away and prepare himself to mark one of the best forwards of all time to the best of his ability. And that's what he did in that final — he held the great corner forward scoreless from play. Mikey had his penalty kick saved by Furlong and scored three frees but otherwise was kept quiet. That was why having Mick around was such a bonus to Offaly. He made himself one of the fittest players in the squad by sheer dedication and while he didn't have the athletic prowess of his brother Pat out on the half back line, he had what Kerry could have done with in the end — a fully paid-up member of the cornerbacks' union who took it as an insult if his opponent got possession, never mind got a score off him.

I first came across him around 1974 when he was brought into that Offaly squad to freshen things up. Even then, he was very consistent and his idea of man-marking was exactly that. He always put the team first whether it was Gracefield or Offaly. He didn't exactly win any popularity contest in Dublin after his flying tackle on Ciaran Duff in the 1983 Leinster Final but that was his reaction to something that had happened to his brother moments earlier.

Pat Fitzgerald — I strongly believe that of all the Offaly lads I played with, Pat Fitzgerald was the one who got the least kudos for the high standard of performances he consistently achieved in the tricolour jersey. He should have seriously been considered for footballer of the year with Furlong in '82 and for years before and even after, he was the one player who didn't let his standards drop.

Pat was a gazelle with even more economical movement across the ground than Liam Currams — and that's saying something. His anticipation was what marked him apart. He was moving to a ball long before anyone knew where it was going. Pat could equally have been at home as a forward or a back because he read the game well and was as safe as houses.

Seán Lowry — Never the fastest as he'd admit himself but he reminded me of Franz Beckenbauer. Someone once said to the German and Bayern Munich captain that he wasn't the fastest man going from A to B. Franz replied that he never started out from A.

Seánie was the same, he was a few moves ahead of everyone else in his head. He had to be because he didn't have the zip that most defenders need to get out of trouble. He was a great footballer and there aren't too many centre-backs who win an All Star as a full forward like Seánie did.

Obviously I have a special affection for this man as we both are the same age and came up through the minor and U-21 ranks together with the county. That in our case was 13 or 14 years together and close observers to the documentaries on the Offaly team of '82 and the one on myself will see there was plenty of banter from him when my goal was mentioned.

Seánie was much more than just a player — you couldn't but like him. He had substance. I mean the more you think about it, the more you realise the leadership qualities he had inside our dressing-room.

Liam Currams — I have a special regard for this man because of the welcome he gave me when I returned to the squad. Liam is one of only a small handful of players who holds All-Ireland medals in hurling and football and is also an All-

Star in both codes. When Kerry speed was a serious problem for opposing defences, his promotion into the Offaly set-up became a real boost. He could run like the wind and that was important in the way he could get back to reclaim possession while his pace put us on the front foot when he went forward.

He set the tone for Offaly's performance in the final by getting that first point but he also played really well throughout the game. He was a tower of strength and when you looked around the dressing room and saw he was in your colours, you knew that his pace was an asset that could change a game. No one ever mentions his contributions late in the '82 final, but he picked up an amount of ball and laid it off to better placed players with simple hand-passes.

Tomás O'Connor — He got an All-Star following his tremendous showing in the Leinster semi-final against Dublin in Portlaoise in 1978. That was a day when he destroyed no less a player than Brian Mullins by plucking balls out of the clouds.

Yet it would be inaccurate to say that Tomás was that sort of player. In fact, if anything, I would describe him as another of our 'unsung hero' brigade who got through a huge volume of unseen work in every game. When I look at videos of some of our old matches, I've given up counting the amount of times you'd see Tomás making a tackle which would have gone almost unnoticed on first viewing. He showed his character for the All-Ireland final in 1981 when he shouldn't have played because of the injury he was carrying. Offaly was in a mini-crisis going into that game and it was important that he lined out — even if he couldn't move as well as normal. His work ethic in every match was a given because he was such an honest player and like his brother Liam, he got the very best out of himself.

Padge Dunne — He was the force of nature Offaly needed to push on from being there or thereabouts to actually becoming winners. He has the biggest hands on a man since Pat Jennings and his long arms meant he could reach to the sky and effortlessly secure high balls. What was even more of a bonus to the panel was the way he breezed into the set up as the youngest player but thought, acted and played like he was a veteran.

Later when both of us got into the same pub game, we helped each other out any way we could and consequently have become very close friends. This guy is no slouch in the slagging stakes either and if you listen to him, you could be slightly confused whether it was himself or myself who scored that winning goal!

John Guinan — When you look at that forward line Offaly put out in the All-Ireland final, John was the person most likely to be replaced. His job was to make sure Offaly didn't lose the game by allowing Kerry players bomb up the pitch creating overlaps. In the event of a tight game when Offaly needed to win, bringing an extra scorer on for him made sense.

John was 20 in that final, only a few months older than Padge, but even at that stage of his development, he had real power and pace and was also happy to work like a Trojan.

Guinan was Richie's lieutenant, he was there to throw himself around and leave the scoring to others. That Kerry halfback line was a major influence in games with Páidí, Tim and Tommy behaving as if they were an alternate half-forward line.

It's well known that Richie was put there to do a job — Guinan also was briefed to make it a really physical encounter.

If you think about it, the selectors made the right decision in taking John off not because he wasn't contributing — remember he had just won a free as I came on the pitch to replace him — but because with a little less than seven minutes left, the Offaly forward line needed a scorer to win the game.

That's not saying John couldn't score. The reality is that without him we wouldn't have got out of the Leinster semi-final game against Laois in Tullamore with a win. He scored 1-1 and those scores were the difference on the day when Laois were every bit as good as us, if not a bit better. He also scored three points in the Leinster Final against Dublin in the following match so he was one of those players who could finish but by the time the final came around we had Matt, Brendy and Johnny doing that end of the job.

It was very much a 'horses-for-courses' situation against Kerry and John was a key man tasked with defending from the front. His work-rate was prodigious in that game and I'm not exaggerating when I tell you that once you got a belt of his powerful body during a game, you knew about it for the rest of the day.

Himself and Mick Lowry were the two players taken off in the final but these guys were stalwarts of the team and while people would think they mightn't have contributed that much because they were replaced, the squad members know how important they were to us.

Richie Connor — The fact that he was Offaly captain and I was the one who scored the winning goal meant both of us got invitations to attend countless functions together over the years. Originally Richie and my brother, Stephen, would have been pals because they are the same age, went to college together and played underage together for Offaly.

I'd mostly have had contact with him when Walsh Island played Rhode because more often than not, I was stuck on him.

Richie had this amazing presence in a dressing room. He was such a big man that he almost blocked out daylight behind him. I don't particularly remember anything he ever said as Offaly captain, but I do remember always thinking: "Thank God this fella is playing with me today."

From the beginning, Eugene had no doubts but he was the one to lead Offaly. He was the trusted deputy that the manager bounced ideas off. They even travelled together to Arsenal in an effort to steal a march on other GAA county teams to find out the best and most up-to-date ways to prepare for games.

Richie had an easy-going manner, loved social company and certainly knew how to enjoy himself. He was popular because he never took the piss out of anyone more than himself. I remember him one time telling an audience that when he came into the Offaly squad initially, he was introduced as Murt Connor's brother. By the time he left, he was known as Matt Connor's brother.

We were lucky with that Offaly squad that we had players who arguably were the most versatile group playing at the time. Richie played full-back, centre-back, midfield and centre-forward. Whenever McGee felt there was a problem, Richie was his Red Adair.

There is no doubt that the way Tim Kennelly galvanised the Kerry team was the defining reason why they won easily enough in 1981. Our manager made the decision that such a performance would not happen on his watch again.

Richie's influence in defence was sacrificed so that he could do a job — albeit a very negative one — for the sake of the team. How can we measure the importance of that move in setting the foundation for our victory?

In my opinion, it was a major contributing factor, as his physicality not only matched the Kerry No 6, but eclipsed it on the day. He probably forfeited an All-star at centre-back that year. There's no more to be said when you do a thing like that. He sacrificed his own game for Offaly so that the county could win the match.

Gerry Carroll — Didn't have a great game in the final and we still slag him that he didn't score that day. He helped change the game though when he and Richie moved out to the middle of the park after Kerry had gained a stranglehold there in the third quarter. He helped change the flow which got us on the ball so that we could get up the field and gets scores.

Gerry oozed class with that educated left foot of his. He was tremendously versatile and often was the go-to man when we needed an injection in midfield or further in. Probably his best day in an Offaly jersey was when he scored 2-1 against Kerry in the All-Ireland semi-final in 1980 on the day Matt scored 2-9 and we lost by 4-15 to 4-10, the two boys our only scorers in the game.

Gerry is long since domiciled in the United States and I always look him up when I go there. As an Edenderry man, he used to call into me a lot when I had a shop in the town and we had many chats about football long before we both won our 1982 Celtic Crosses together.

Gerry was a fantastic athlete on the pitch and a decent guy off it. He is the type that if he could do you a good turn, he would be happy to do so.

Johnny Mooney — He was one of the most complete footballers I ever witnessed yet I honestly believe we never saw the best of him. I know he is a club man of my own but he had so much athletic and football talent that he could have been one of the great midfielders, up there with Mick O'Connell, Willie Bryan, Mick Carley... that type of player who could fly through the air to field a ball.

If he had been as dedicated as the likes of Stephen, there would be no one that I can think of who could have played him. What a natural talent. McGee maintained that we wouldn't have won the All-Ireland without him and I totally agree with that assertion. It is to the manager's credit that he knew how to handle Gerry Carroll and Johnny, who weren't maybe as straightforward to deal with as the others. It wasn't that they didn't take their football seriously because they did. They were younger and less orthodox than the rest of us. And they had a level of self-belief that was vital for other members of the squad to be around.

Both were immensely gifted footballers — and they knew it. And because of that, we knew it and we took it into the group as a major plus because they were a part of us.

In any squad, there are several personality types — some just get on with it, others are fine with a bit of managing and then there might be two or three others who can make or break a group, depending on how they are handled.

They require a different type of man-management and I give McGee 10 out of 10 for the way he performed that role.

If you think of '82 when we were trying to hang on to Kerry, Mooney was winning ball, got two points as well and over the 70 minutes probably won every ball he went for.

Matt Connor — He burst on the scene scoring 3-2 in Askeaton against Limerick when just out of minor ranks. That was the good thing about McGee, he didn't care what age you were if you could do the job. That same day a young lad from Tullamore, Mickey White scored 1-4 and he was from the same Offaly minor team as Matt. He opted for soccer though and was a huge loss because he was top class. That was only Matt's second league game for Offaly but from then on he changed in the public eye to being 'Matt The Thresher.' Everyone loved him, even fans of opposing teams. The reason he rose above county boundaries was because of the class he brought to a game. For a big strong man, he had the grace and balance of a ballerina.

Younger GAA fans got their first chance to see just what Matt had to offer when the documentaries on Offaly and on myself were recently released. I'm living down in Toomevara in Co Tipperary and many of the people who come into the pub said they had never seen him play. They had heard about him but when they saw him in those clips on TG4, their eyes were opened. He was a man who could score off either foot and was only in his mid-twenties when he finished playing. He was a genius. We won't ever see a better forward than Matt.

Only recently I was talking about DJ (Carey) and Henry Shefflin. Such players are worth 10 to 12 points to a team. Matt was the same to us. Mick O'Dwyer said something that was a great statement in my estimation: "That Offaly side came with Matt Connor and went with Matt Connor."

What a loss he was to us and not just that squad but imagine the young lads coming in to the Offaly set-up for the following six or seven years if they had Matt to look up to and his influence to spread around in training and in match situations.

People mightn't realise it but mentally Matt was really strong and pressure didn't faze him. Looking back, I suppose it was that strength that has helped him in life since the accident that confined him to a wheelchair since Christmas in 1984. I see he retired this year after being a Guard for over 40 years... what a man, what a player, what an inspiration. An honour to have played with him.

Brendan Lowry — I rated Brendy very highly. He was an out-and-out striker, who despatched scores with the minimum of fuss. He was so good that the odd time he missed, you'd be shocked. He got three points in the final and actually kicked the first score of the game but it was disallowed for a foul out the field.

No matter who marked him, and there were some great corner backs around at that time, he would always get important scores.

Brendy had this uncanny ability of being able to find a pocket of space and that was all he needed. In similar situations other forwards would have to make runs into space or be given more time on the ball. If you ever watch those old games, you will be astonished by his economy of movement. He could catch and despatch almost in one movement. Most of his points just got over the bar — he wasn't one for blazing high balls in his attempt at scoring. The trajectory he chose took the wind factor out of the equation and when it came to goals, he was lethal. I don't know whether it was the 'eyes' he gave the goalkeepers or the power he got into his shot, but his efforts invariably ended up in the back of the net.

Brendy was also a really good soccer player and we can be thankful in Offaly that he joined the squad because he enjoyed playing with Ferbane Town. I think when Seánie and Mick were on the county panel, it made it easier for him to commit from 1980 onwards. There is no doubt he was a link we needed to win because without him, there would have been too much weight put on Matt's shoulders both to win possession and score from the inside line.

What McGee wanted me to do was drop deep out of the

full-forward line so that both those guys had room to run into it. I only got the chance beside them in the Leinster Final against Dublin and a few challenge games. When I got injured, Eugene got Matt to play the role leaving Brendy and Mooney to quarry scores. Five points between them and I'd say another five came off them through 'assists' or direct fouls on them.

Brendy was also a smashing guy to have around the squad. He had a great sense of mischief and was well able to cut down anyone who got too big for his boots. When I see how great his son Shane has done on the golf circuit, I'm not surprised. Accuracy was Brendy's middle name.

Ollie Minnock — Ollie got injured just before the final. He broke his ankle. What a defender; he had a good head, good hands and always seemed to win his own ball.

He was such a top footballer that he played mostly at midfield for his club, Clara, but he was also a good centre back. He started out that season in the first Offaly match against Louth in Croke Park playing at centre-forward. And while he didn't pull up trees, he did well and scored two fine points. I think McGee knew what Ollie could do and was worried that he lacked that little thrust of pace against the likes of Egan or Sheehy. Eugene was planning for Kerry from the start of that year and saw that maybe Ollie could have done a job on Kennelly because Ollie too was well-built and was as strong as a horse. In the end, he got injured and Richie played that relocation role asked of him to perfection.

Liam O'Mahony — He scored three points in the Leinster final, came on again in the Galway game and was a seriously good footballer. Gave the whole panel a lift with the form he produced in training and in matches in the lead up to the All-Ireland final.

Hughie Bolton — He would be the invisible man of our group. He made a huge contribution in bringing players on in training because he was a hardy jigger and he made you honest if you were going for the ball with him. He was a model squad player who didn't throw tantrums because he didn't get to play. Instead he was a guy who always turned up on time and if you told him we were training on the top of Carrauntoohil in the morning, he'd be the first man there.

Dinny Wynne — Was the sub goalie to Furlong and a really good one at that. I felt so sorry for him when he got his chance in '84 against Longford and it didn't work out. He was unfortunate that he was around at the time when one of the greatest goalkeepers of all time was minding the Offaly net.

Charlie Conroy — He started the year before and the year after but was unlucky to lose out in the year we won it. He was close to the team and may have lost out because of his size. In my opinion, Charlie was very unlucky not to start in 1982. He was a fearless defender, a good attacking corner back who gave everything to Offaly when he was picked.

Martin Fitzpatrick — We came into the Offaly panel on the same evening in 1982. I know when the selectors huddled together to see who they'd bring on in the closing stages of the Kerry match, it boiled down to Martin and myself. Eugene proposed me and the others agreed to reverse a decision they all had made the previous night that Martin would go in. I think it was the conditions and the fact that there was so little time left that swung it in my favour.

Aidan O'Halloran — He was the boy wonder of colleges' football with the Carmelite College in Moate and was rated very highly by a lot of good judges. Offaly were rebuilding to mount an assault on the All-Ireland when he relocated with his job to Tullamore and transferred from Westmeath to play with Offaly. Being rivals and neighbouring counties, Aidan took a fair bit of stick over this but in hindsight it was the right decision as he improved the Offaly dressing room and played in some big games.

Unfortunately, he missed out on playing in 1982 against Kerry but he was a factor on several big days. He represented

Offaly for a number of years before relocating to Galway. I'm sure he has developed a big interest in rugby these days as his son, Tiernan, is part of the Connacht team and has played for Ireland.

There were also a number of Offaly lads who were very unlucky not to get an All-Ireland medal in 1982. I feel sorry for the likes of **Gerry Hickey**, **Vinny Henry** and **Pat Doyle** that they missed out after giving years of service. They were three very good footballers. I remember Vinny and Pat did well in the '78 Leinster championship semi-final match against Dublin in Portlaoise. Vinny broke one of the posts that day as Offaly almost shocked Dublin. Vinny started the '81 final in that roving full-forward role that McGee called the 'Vinny Henry role.'

Mick Wright was another great warrior who gave a lot over the years but was missing when we won in 1982. He could have got in as a corner back ahead of Mick Lowry or Stephen, both of whom were really half-backs, but Mick only wanted to play centre-back and McGee saw him as a corner man. The story about him was the selectors were picking a panel for '82 on the bus after a match in Mayo. McGee told Wright that if he played corner back and kicked out the ball he would guarantee him an All-Star. Wright got up and said: "If I'm not centre-back, don't put me on the panel."

John Moran (Tubber), **Sean Lawlor** (Gracefield), **Declan Farrell** (Edenderry) and Daingean's **Joe Rigney** are others who were decidedly unlucky to lose out when they were so close. They had been there that year but when the panel was cut, they were the ones who were dropped following the semi-final win over Galway. I don't understand it myself but seemingly Offaly couldn't carry that big a panel. Nowadays, the GPA wouldn't put up with that, and those lads would have their Celtic Crosses the same as the players and subs who were in the official panel on the day.

Joe was the young lad I ran into on the night I scored that goal against Daingean which was the reason I got back into the Offaly panel. He knocked me back with his force but as I was falling I managed to stick it in the back of the net to force a draw.

I was worried about Joe because he wasn't able to sit the Leaving Certificate that year after the hit he took. They had to pull a door off the dressing-room as a makeshift stretcher to carry him to the ambulance during that game.

Tom Fitzpatrick — I watched Tom come through the ranks and on his day he could blow you away. He was around the Offaly scene for a number of years and made his own contribution but was gone by the time I got back in.

Paschal Healy — He started some championship matches but went off to Australia. I think he was on the panel in early in '82 but left before I returned in the middle of that year.

The management and backroom team

With Eugene McGee, there was a strong backroom staff. Chief of these were his selectorial team of **Seán Foran**, **Paddy Fenlon**, **PJ Mahon** and **Leo Grogan**.

Tom Donoghue had a huge influence on our group. He was, and is, one of a kind. Nominally, Tom, who won a hurling All-Ireland with Offaly, was our trainer but he was much more than that. I think every player saw him as a friend and someone they could confide in. It is testament to the professional way he approached training our panel with Eugene that we were able to outlast that great Kerry team.

We were blessed too in the way **Brian Emerson**, the team doctor, and **Ossie Bennett**, the masseur, looked out for us so well on the medical end. I would also like to salute the memory of the original masseur, **Joe Flanagan**, who turned up for years and gave hundreds of Offaly players good old-fashioned rubs. He was great for his time.

And before I leave this chapter, it is worth noting how important it is in the GAA to be born in the right place from a winning point of view. I say this because **Ollie Crinnigan** came from a place very close to the Offaly border. Had he been born a little bit closer to Edenderry, there would have been some fun between himself and Furlong fighting for that No 1 position.

Stephen Darby — I've written the next chapter about my little brother who has always been a great friend to me except when he marked me that day for Rhode against Edenderry in 1989.

Stephen is very quiet and considered as a person. He'd be inclined to keep things to himself but I'd confide quite a bit in him.

CHAPTER 25

THE OTHER
'SEAMUS DARBY'

We don't look alike in any way but according to my brother Stephen, there are times when he'd be better off just changing his name to Seamus Darby.

Ever since the 1982 final, it's as if he hasn't existed in his own right as a player and instead if he is at a wedding or a function or on holidays in some part of the country, people's memory seems to morph him and myself into the one person.

It's happened so often to him that it's come to the stage that Stephen sees the funny side of these encounters. As he says himself, I can either get annoyed or amused. Having said that, there are times I'm mistaken for Stephen but I do accept that he has the greater cross to bear when these mix-ups occur.

These occurrences invariably start out with someone saying: "Is that your man Darby over there?" Then someone will approach and ask for an autograph or a picture. Luckily, Stephen hasn't a jealous bone in his body and this whole 'Darby thing' has brought us closer over the years instead of driving a wedge between us.

In fact, the pair of us were always pals and did things together around and outside of the house from the time he was old enough to talk and walk. We slept in the one bed all our lives growing up, as he was the next born brother to me. We were the two big lads in the house and our job was to help Daddy on the bog or making hay or whatever farm job was in season.

Stephen is very quiet and considered as a person. He'd be inclined to keep things to himself but I'd confide quite a bit in him. It's unusual enough to see brothers so close but the two of us always have a similar set of friends from our Offaly days — Richie, Padge, John Guinan, myself and himself we'd knock around a fair bit together.

We were all on that same Offaly panel and there are several other lads we'd be friendly with when we were playing. I suppose the friendship thing got deeper when both Padge and myself went in to the same line of business by opening pubs.

He launched 'Dunne's After Dark' in Portarlington and I had my own place down in Toomevara. That meant if I had a function on, Padge and Richie and some of the lads would come down and support me and if there was something on in his premises, myself and Stephen would go to Portarlington.

Public houses operate very much from evening into night time nowadays unlike when I was young and a premises would be open from 10 o'clock in the morning and then had strict closing times at 11pm (winter) or 11.30 pm in summertime.

People come out later and stay later in the modern culture so it means that once you have cleaned up and got the barrels in order for the next day, you can have large chunks of the morning and afternoon to yourself.

There was a period of time when Richie worked away from the classroom as well which allowed the three of us, and Stephen during his summer holidays, to meet up for a game of golf.

You'd be surprised how many invitations former players get to support various charities and all of us would feel a duty to give something back to communities whether it was for a GAA golf day or one a club or county board might be organising for one reason or another.

As those of you who play golf know, it is a frustrating game if you want to try to hit the ball like a Shane Lowry. At our level, we'd try and be competitive but never at the expense of a bit of craic. Often at those occasions, none of us would take a drink either because we had to get back to work in the bar or because nowadays there is a big responsibility on everyone not to drink and drive. If we knew in advance that we were staying late, then we'd get a lift to the golf course or book into a local hotel overnight.

The four of us would more often than not decide to play in these events and as a result have spent a lot of time in each other's company. At this stage there isn't too much we don't know about each other's lives — good and bad.

Stephen and I may be as unalike as chalk and cheese but ever since he arrived in the world a few days after Christmas in 1954, I, as his big brother, have felt a strong bond with him.

While we both always loved football as young lads growing up, Stephen was way more assiduous than me when it came to the books and studying. So as I made my way in the world in a variety of jobs before becoming a rep on the road, he did the Leaving Certificate and in time qualified as a national teacher. As he showed in his time in Ballybryan National School as principal, he was a person who became a leader in his own community and was looked up to for the wise counsel and advice he gave both parents and pupils.

That's where we were different. As the eldest, I suppose I felt there was more pressure on me to contribute to our burgeoning family and was happy to ditch school at the first opportunity and start bringing home some money for my mother. During those years I went from job to job and Stephen began studying in Dublin. Football was the common interest that kept us close at a time when other brothers who didn't play might be drifting apart.

No life ever runs smoothly all the time but as I said when trouble came to our doors, we were there for each other. It is one of the saddest times in my memory when Stephen's first wife, Betty, tragically died at the age of 23 from leukemia. He was bereft at the time and we can only be thankful that Carmel came along to bring joy back into his life. They are a wonderful couple with three boys, two of whom — Brian and Niall –followed in his footsteps by playing for Offaly. Indeed Niall still is while Brian, who followed his father as principal in the same school, retired last year after giving sterling service for well over a decade to the Faithful cause.

The fact that Stephen and myself played football together for Rhode and Offaly means we have many shared memories which makes our relationship all the more special. As quiz experts know, we became the first two brothers ever to come on in an All-Ireland final and winning in 1982 for me was all the more special because my brother was on the field with me.

While I'm no giant myself at 5'8" (if that), Stephen is only 5'5" and not many players his size make it onto the county scene. Knowing him, I think he decided that he was going to get on the Offaly team and nothing was ever going to stop him — certainly not his size.

However, I remember one night when he was about 21 in 1976, he suffered such a horrific injury that I wondered if he would ever walk properly again, never mind play Gaelic football at the highest level. He got the injury during a tournament game Rhode played one midweek evening in Abbeyleix.

I can still see what happened as if it was yesterday. Stephen went down over a ball with his legs spread out and one of their lads rushed in and in trying to get the ball, just fell on top of him. It was as simple as that.

I was right beside him when it happened and could immediately see he was in serious trouble. The pain was excruciating and the roars out of him were something fierce. Daddy, who was at the match, ran onto the pitch and was over to us in seconds and we both tried to soothe Stephen in his obvious discomfort. The game was stopped for several minutes before Daddy and myself got either side of him and carried him out to the car.

What were we going to do with him? There seemed no point in bringing him to a hospital as it was late and there were no physios much operating around that time. As we were in county Laois, we decided that we'd head straight across to Myshall in Carlow and visit Dan O'Neill.

Dan became famous as the owner of the great horse Danoli many years later but at the time there was a mystique around him as a bonesetter for both animals and humans. People swore by him and no matter what time of the day or night you pulled up in his yard, there was a queue.

I drove the 35 miles across country as carefully as I could because every bump in the road was agony for Stephen. We arrived in to Dan's place approaching nine o'clock in the evening. I could see ahead of us there were farmers holding cattle by their halters and a few horse-boxes with trainers standing outside waiting their turn.

Dan was in full flow treating them all and I estimated it would be a few hours before he got to see us. By the time our turn came, it was approaching midnight and Stephen's knee had swollen up like a balloon by then.

The difference between playing today and in our day four decades ago was that we would even contemplate coming to a place like this for diagnosis and treatment. For a start this wasn't a bone problem, yet we had come to a bonesetter, albeit one of great renown. If such a potential cruciate injury occurred in the present day, the immediate medical advice would be to get an MRI once the area had been well-iced to allow the swelling to go down. Then after a few weeks, the player would know if he needed an operation and if he did, he would begin to slowly build up the knee so that he could play again. I've heard of people getting back as quickly as seven months nowadays but the norm is probably nine months to a year.

Looking at Stephen that night and seeing how immobile the whole knee area had become, the worry that crossed my mind was that he might never have proper use of it again.

Dan had his own way of doing things — no doubt because a lot of his treatments were carried out on animals. When our turn came, without any warning, he caught Stephen by the leg and straightened up his knee in one powerful movement.

Not expecting such a quick start to his examination, Stephen went white as the pain shot through him like an electric shock. Seconds later, Dan repeated the process. How Stephen didn't pass out I'll never know.

However successful Dan may have been with the cattle and horses that night, his methods didn't work for Stephen. For days and weeks afterwards, he was in a desperate discomfort and unable to put any weight on the leg. In fact, he spent months just hobbling around.

Around that time in the mid-seventies, I don't think anyone knew what that injury was that Stephen suffered. Indeed it wasn't until Pat Spillane picked up a similar injury that journalists began to put a name on it. Nowadays every club seems to deal with players having their cruciate done a number of times per year. It is still a terrible injury to get but it's not career threatening as it was when Stephen suffered it.

He missed a year of his footballing career because of the knee injury he suffered that evening in Abbeyleix. Never once though did he concede that it would impede his progress to achieving his aims of playing with Offaly. He approached his rehabilitation with a single-minded determination to build his knee up so that he could get back to play for the club. In the Power Station in Rhode, somebody there who was interested in football and knew of his plight designed a crude-looking exercise boot made out of iron. This was a very heavy contraption to wear but Stephen had it on constantly and I've my suspicion that he even wore it to bed. He was totally concentrated on strengthening the affected knee area and devised a set of exercises himself to speed up the process.

If I had got that cruciate injury, I know for sure I would never have had the patience or the understanding to do what he did. It would have ended my career.

Stephen was different and plotted his own medical recovery. He was clever enough to allow all the swelling to go down before building up the knee and while he wore a knee strapping afterwards, he managed to get back to full speed and within a year was playing championship football in the Rhode colours. We got as far as the 1977 Offaly semi-final where we lost to Daingean by a point 0-10 to 0-9. I should have scored a goal in that game but didn't place the ball properly and their goalkeeper, Christy Todd, turned the ball away brilliantly. I was disappointed with that as once I was clear of the defence, I'd always expect myself to put the ball away. Daingean in turn lost the final to Tullamore who completed a remarkable treble — minor, U-21 and senior title wins that year.

Any talk of 'Darby' in those years was about Stephen because after overcoming that terrible setback, he slowly began to get better and better as Offaly went about lowering Dublin's colours in Leinster. It became a source of great satisfaction to me that when I was no longer on the panel after 1977 that I could go and watch my brother playing for the county. When you are close like Irish GAA families are, it's almost as if you are playing because of the satisfaction you get from victories and the pain you suffer with defeats.

I'm talking about a time in the late seventies when there were two powerhouse teams — Dublin and Kerry in the country — and the rest were nowhere.

Each year though, Offaly developed thanks to McGee's meticulous plotting and planning. Beaten by Wexford in '77, they put it up to Dublin in Portlaoise in '78 without Stephen seeing action. They then lost a Leinster Final they should have won in '79 when he was Offaly's star outfield player with Furlong also playing a blinder. That was the day Jimmy Keaveney got sent off but Offaly allowed a lead to slip to the 14-man Dubs and lost to a sucker punch goal from Bernard Brogan in the last minute.

I thought that might act as a real setback to the team and certainly it gave rise to plenty of reshuffling on the selectors' front. However, once Offaly got the bit between their teeth again the following summer, they got back on the title winning trail by beating Dublin with a powerful second-half display in that 1980 Leinster Final. Stephen didn't play in that match but he was very much part of the panel and the arrival of Liam Currams out of minor meant there were about seven top class players looking for a half-back position — Mick Wright, Richie and Seánie in the centre and Pat Fitzgerald, Charlie Conroy, Liam and Stephen for the wings.

Currams was one of these forces of nature who come along every so often. Despite his tender years, he had to be accommodated while when fit, I don't think Pat Fitzgerald has ever played below an 8-rating.

The fact that Stephen was in contention and I remember he played a number of matches between the championship games, kept our family interest on a personal level.

The nearest I got to kick a ball in those barren years on the inter-county front was through Stephen. I remember how proud we all were when I got nominated for an All Star award in 1976. Three years later Stephen had a magnificent year and if anything, we were even prouder of what he had achieved, given the way he had to fight back to fitness.

He was so good in 1979 that the local paper made him Offaly's best championship player at a time when Furlong, Mooney, Kilmurray and the Connors were playing out of their skins.

What encapsulated this form for me was watching the great David Hickey of Dublin having to resort to pulling and dragging Stephen as he made his way up the field under the Hogan Stand in the Leinster Final. Here was a 5'5" man taking the fight to a much bigger opponent and forcing him to foul if he wanted to stop him.

I've since got it on impeccable authority that Stephen was the closest a player ever got to an All Star without actually winning one. Seemingly those meetings are a series of checks and balances and while he was selected in one check, he lost out at the very end to Danny Murray of Roscommon, who was another fabulous player in that position.

I'm convinced he would have nailed down a place on the

team on foot of those displays except he suffered a similar, but more serious knee injury in a league game against Kildare played in November 1979.

Stephen had just married Betty, who was terminally ill at the time (and died a few months later in January), on the Saturday. She suggested that he should play the game the following day. He was going for a ball near the Offaly goal with his man when Martin Furlong advanced and hit him inadvertently with the full force of his two knees.

The upshot was that Stephen severed the medial ligaments on that same knee and was out of action for another nine months. He got back for the All-Ireland semi-final in '81. It is an injury that has forced him to have six operations later in life and there is no doubt it militated against him establishing himself in the Offaly defence in '81 and '82.

I have two standout memories in which Stephen and myself played together. One was the county final we won against Daingean (1-12 to 1-7) in 1975 when we both lined out either side of our great friend, Gerry Hickey, on the Rhode half-forward line. I was 24 and Stephen was 20 at the time. We often joke that of the 1-12 scored by Rhode in O'Connor Park that day, the half-forward line was responsible for all but two points which came from Jody Gunning and Tom Darcy.

The truth is that Gerry gave an incredible performance, scoring all of the remaining 1-10 by himself. Myself and Stephen were the hod-carriers that afternoon but it was a great occasion for the Darby family, particularly my father Christy, to see the two of us on a Dowling Cup-winning team.

I think that particular day was playing around a little in my head on the other big occasion when the two of us were on the field and had just won another title. That was, of course, September 19, 1982, when we beat Kerry.

When the final whistle blew, the first thing I wanted to do was to find Stephen and hug him and congratulate him. People don't realise that in those last minutes as Kerry went scurrying for a score of any kind, it was Stephen who 'cut' the ball out of Tom Spillane's hand as he tried to break through.

That stopped the momentum and although, there was still the chance of a score because the ball was close to our goal, Martin Furlong rode to the rescue single-handedly got the ball away from the danger area. Kerry won possession again and Mikey Sheehy kicked a high ball across our goal. Seánie caught it, dummied past a player and then began celebrating when he heard the final whistle sound.

What a tsunami of emotions greeted that whistle — we were in ecstasy while Kerry were shattered and in total despair. The Offaly crowd were delirious and within seconds the Croke Park pitch was full of enthusiastic supporters giving first vent to a famous victory.

I wanted to get down to Stephen because I knew giving away the penalty would have been weighing on his mind and I wanted him to have a positive memory of what had been achieved by the team.

However the crowd enveloped all the Offaly players so quickly that it was virtually impossible to move, never mind get down the 100 yards between us. Total bedlam ensued for 10 or 15 minutes and we had no choice but to go with the flow being created. Everyone was elated and so was I.

They lifted me up, I remember Johnny Mooney and Seánie were being chaired across to the Hogan Stand to get ready for the presentation.

It was when I got near the Hogan Stand that I saw Stephen. We smiled at each other, hugged and I told him how he had saved us. I can remember at that moment actually thinking to myself: "Seamus, this is fairytale stuff. Enjoy every last second of it. And I did."

Like probably most sports-mad families, Stephen and myself had been playing All-Irelands around the house all our lives and now here we were together. For real. Getting to live the dreams of our youth. We were both All-Ireland winners against Kerry waiting for the President of the GAA, Paddy Buggy from Kilkenny to present the cup to Richie.

I'd been on these steps before as an unused substitute in '71 and as someone who played the whole match and scored two points in the '72 replay against Kerry. Despite that, I'd felt I was very much a peripheral figure. This was totally different. There was the Kerry factor, preventing history being made and the drama of a late goal that I had been fortunate enough to score.

More importantly, I was there winning with my brother beside me and because of the goal, it was obvious that along with Furlong's save, I was one of the central figures on this occasion.

That would sink in more and more as the months and years progressed. Right then, in the moment we were still togged out and collecting the Sam Maguire, my thoughts were totally around my family and Stephen and myself winning medals together.

There was another time when we were close together on a pitch but the context was totally different to that day in Croke Park. It was about seven years later, in 1989 when I had taken over as trainer of Edenderry and had switched to play with them as well. As luck would have it, we met Rhode in the semi-final of the Offaly senior football championship.

The first game ended in a draw and with Jody Gunning over Rhode, I knew the way he would be thinking for the replay — and I was right. Rhode put Stephen marking me from the start of that match. I knew well that I was in deep trouble whatever the outcome but sure what could I do, only play my best and leave the rest to fate.

It was truly a weird feeling running down into my corner forward position before the start of the game in Tullamore and my brother taking his place beside me. We have played so many times together for Rhode that neither of us had to look up to know where the other would be when we had the ball. Stephen always played with intelligence and his anticipation made up for whatever he lacked in size. Now here we were joined at the hip marking each other.

In such moments, thoughts run through your head because you know him better than anyone and you know he knows you through and through as well. We both can be bitter and totally focused in match situations. There was no hugging this time. No smiles. No greetings. We just about gave each other the most miserable handshake ever but neither of us said 'good luck' to the other.

It was a sweltering summer's day when the ball was thrown in and there was no quarter asked or given by any of the 30 players on the pitch. This was a 'derby game' as well as a 'Darby game.'

As I explained earlier, my father hated everyone in Edenderry — but only in a GAA way. That was the stew I was in after throwing my lot in with Edenderry for 1989. Idi Amin would have got a warmer welcome from my father if he had called to his door.

There was a huge build-up — this just wasn't club against club any more but a family against itself. Ours. It got to the other players on both sides so by the time the game started, it was war.

I can still see the dust rising around the Rhode goalmouth after a high ball landed and both sets of players were fighting for possession. About five or six fellas went flying in at the one time. It was manic stuff due to the burning desire of every player to win the ball.

I got so caught up watching this incident that I didn't notice where Stephen was. The next thing I see him running in from behind the tussle, rising the ball and heading away from goal. Two red jerseys tried to block him coming out — pulling and dragging a bit like Hickey did in Croke Park. I'd say I was 30 yards away but I could see clearly the determination on his face which made him unbeatable when he was in the groove.

He then jinked away from another Edenderry forward who

In action during the second-half of the Leinster Final against Dublin in 1982. I got my leg bandaged at half-time after pulling my hamstring late in the first half.

With Veronne and our newly born son Shay at the Coombe Hospital in October 1982.

The great Johnny Geraghty, Jody Gunning and myself discussing the game as we relaxed with a drink.

Above: Five brothers, Seán, Tomás, Michael, myself and Stephen.

Right: Myself and Pat Delaney, the great Offaly hurling centre back in New York, 1983.

Left: Competing in the 1982 Milk Superstars.

Below: With George Best in 1984.

Veronne and
our son Shay.

Myself and our
son Ryan.

Veronne
and myself
relaxing at
home after
Shay was
born in 1982.

Naomi and myself pose for a photo.

My son
Ryan on
his way to
school.

Veronne, myself and our three children on Shay's First Communion day.

Myself and son Ryan.

Myself and my mother Janie.

My mother, Eileen, myself and Mary with David and Sinead Farrell.

Above: Behind the bar at the Red Lion, London.

Left: Pulling a pint for the late Ger Ryan Snr in the pub in Toomevara.

Eight senior All-Ireland winners in Rhode (back row, left to right): Paddy McCormack, Jody Gunning, Eugene Mulligan, Martin Heavey, myself. Seated are Stephen, Johnny Mooney and Charlie Conroy.

The Darby clan gather for one of life's happy occasions, a family wedding.

The original Darby family (back row, left to right):
Michael, Stephen, Tomás, myself and Sean. Front: Ann,
my father Christy and mother Janie, Mary and Eileeen.

Myself, my son Shay and my two grandchildren Jonah and Kyran.

Gathering of the clan for my parents' 50th anniversary in 1994
Back row, left to right: Kevin Farrell, Michael Darby, Carmel Darby,
Veronne Darby, Ber Darby, Nigel Mooney, Trevor Darby, Mary Mooney,
Wayne Mooney, Ryan Darby, Seán Darby, Seamus Young, Shay Darby,
Ann Young, Eileen Farrell, Tomás Darby and myself.
Seated: Stephen Darby with Christine on his knee, my father Christy
and mother Janie, who has Jenny on her knee, Sinead Farrell, Carmel
Darby with Jason on her knee.
Front row: Joey Darby, David Farrell, Niall Darby, Brian Darby, Lisa
Darby and Steve Darby.

Four
generations
of Darbys
— myself,
my father
Christy, my
son Shay
and his son
Jonah.

With Fr Brian D'Arcy and the late Jimmy Magee.

With Martin
Furlong (above);
and with Brian
Stynes at
Melbourne
Cricket Ground
in 2013 (left).

With the late, great Sean Purcell (left), the former Galway legend.

Below: With Michael Duignan, Bernard Flynn, DJ Carey and Dessie Farrell in Dallas, Texas in 2013.

With Padge Dunne, Richie Connor, Willie Bryan, Nudie Hughes at a golf outing in Castleblayney.

Approaching the top of Carrauntoohil, Ireland's highest mountain, in 2008.

With Mick O'Dwyer (right) and Shane MacGowan (below). I've been lucky enough to meet some great people down the years.

Receiving a medal to mark the 25th anniversary of the victory over Kerry by former GAA President Nickey Brennan at the GAA Jubilee Awards.

It's always great to meet with former teammates, but there is also great fun to be had when you meet former opponents. Here I am with Kerry's goalkeeper from the 1982 final, Charlie Nelligan (right) and the great Eoin 'Bomber' Liston (below).

Johnny Flaherty, myself, Martin Hanamy, Sean Lowry, Kieran Rigney, Michael Duignan, Brendan Clarke, Willie Bryan, Hubert Rigney and Vincent Henry in Croke Park in 2015 to announce Offaly GAA's plans to develop a new centre of excellence.

At the launch of TG4's *Laochra Gael* series at the Dean Hotel in Dublin.

tried to ambush him, creating a mini sandstorm as he barged past.

In the heat of the moment, I yelled out "Stephen" at the top of my voice. That was all we ever needed to let each other know where we were. Without breaking stride, he placed the ball so perfectly on my chest that I hadn't to move a muscle to secure possession.

Luckily for him I was closed down immediately and had to rush my shot which went wide. It would be something of an understatement to say that Stephen wasn't best pleased that I had conned him in that moment. Instinctively, he had followed the habit of a lifetime to give me a pass when I called his name for the ball. His face was like thunder and I felt bad straight away.

He was perfectly within his rights to give me a skelp the next ball we went for together but that wasn't his nature. Instead, he redoubled his efforts and went for every ball as if his life depended on it. I knew I had to do the same or I wouldn't get a kick. The local newspaper report of the match said Stephen did a good job marking me and when it came to who played best for Edenderry, I was included. I'd say we ended up 50-50 on the personal battle, which was about right for the honour of all concerned.

The big mill people expected never materialised but it turned into an intriguing game of football. Edenderry went down by a point 0-13 to 2-6, but Rhode in turn lost out to Ferbane in the final, so there were no medals for any of the Darby clan that year.

That's been as near Stephen and I ever came to falling out on a football pitch or anywhere else for that matter. Together we've shared some great moments down the decades — and some hilarious ones as well.

Now I'm not trying to blow my own trumpet here by saying that thanks to all the publicity about the goal and what it means in the GAA, people often ask me to stand in for photos.

Sometimes they think Stephen is me and ask him by mistake. When he points out who he actually is, they normally say sorry and walk away.

The other Offaly lads, who know both of us well, give him a terrible ribbing any time they are around and something like that happens. I wasn't there myself but the boys told me the day Eugene McGee got married to Marian O'Connor, they had a great time jeering Stephen. It was the year after Offaly won the All-Ireland — 1983 — and Eugene invited all the lads who had been on the panel from the beginning of his time in Offaly. Stephen was there, Martin Furlong, Seánie, Richie, Matt, that group. I was invited to the 'afters' but unfortunately was a road rep working up in Donegal that week and couldn't get back for it.

However, I was at Eugene's stag a few weeks earlier which we held in Rhode in honour of the cursed Clonin Hill that nearly killed us running up and down but which made winners of us too in the way we prepared for the Kerry match.

It was a great night's fun in Mooney's Pub and I'd say it was four o'clock in the morning before we emerged from the premises — everyone well tanked. As I said before, nights like this, when you are in the company of fellas you have been in the trenches with, are precious moments to be savoured. That particular night I realised how much that group meant and would continue to mean to me for the rest of my life.

I could sense others thinking the same. Mick Fitzgerald was one of the really sensible lads in the squad; he would sometimes take the training if Eugene or Tom Donoghue were absent for one reason or another. He was well thought of by the whole group. What stood out for me that night on the footpath outside the pub was the fact that he didn't want it to end and was wondering where we might get 'one for the road'.

A few weeks later without me, the boys reconvened at the wedding and had congregated up around the bar in the Bridge House in Tullamore. As is often the case, other people would approach for a chat or autograph and the lads were always happy to oblige. After the meal when they resumed their chat at the bar, a guy sidled over to Stephen and tapped him on the shoulder.

When Stephen turned around, the man pointed to his wife and two kids sitting at a nearby table and said: "Excuse me, Seamus, would you mind standing in for a photo with me and the family?"

That immediately brought subdued giggles from the other players. Ever polite, Stephen explained as quietly as he could to the man: "No problem but just so you know, I'm not Seamus, I'm Stephen, his brother."

The other person was by now clearly embarrassed and muttered a 'sorry' as he shook Stephen's hand before going back to wife and children to explain that they had the wrong Darby.

By that stage the teasing at the counter was gathering pace as the lads pulled Stephen's leg about how great it must be to have a famous brother. Just when it appeared to be tapering off, the same man comes back up and beckons to Stephen again.

"Listen, I want to apologise again for the mix-up," he said very genuinely. "Someone told me you were Seamus and I took his word for it. I hope I haven't caused you any bother?"

Stephen assured him that it wasn't an issue and just as he was leaving again, he turned right in front of the other Offaly lads, and said: "I suppose Stephen you are the one in the family like myself who never kicked a ball in your life?"

The boys all laughed, agreeing immediately, that he wouldn't be able to kick a ball out of his way — and that was the wind up for Stephen for the rest of the evening.

There was another time when we were at the wedding of Jody Gunning's daughter. This was a big Offaly wedding and you'd expect that everyone would have known the players at the reception.

We had the lovely meal and then Stephen went up to the counter to get a round for the four of us. He brought the women down their drinks and went back up to get our two pints. After paying for the drinks, he had the pints in his hands and was about to come back to our table when a lad from the other end of the county caught him for a chat.

Often what will happen in such a case is you have a few words and move on. I was watching Stephen nodding as the man kept speaking, saw Stephen looking down every now and again at the two pints and still no sign of the other fella drawing breath.

Those who know Stephen would tell you that he'd be very civil and deferential in such circumstances. And he was. So much so that by the time he arrived back, the two points had nearly gone off.

"That seemed like a great chat," I said just hopping the ball in his direction.

"Aye," Stephen replied with a sort of smirk on his face. "All about Offaly and never forgetting that great day. And at the very end do you know what he asked me?"

"No," I answered, "What?"

"Did you get to go to the game yourself or did you watch it on the television?"

After taking a few sips of the stale Guinness your man had ruined with all his chat, Stephen turned to me and said: "Remind me not to go anywhere with you again."

For sure, he has had to put with a lot of that sort of thing down the years. By now, he is well used to it and is able to see the funny side of being my brother.

CHAPTER 26

RHODE — FOR AND AGAINST

I had many great years playing for Rhode from '67 when I was 16 on the bench to '86 when I played my last senior match after 20 seasons in the green and gold colours.

Three county title wins is small return in that time but we came close in other finals without getting across the line. The 'one that got away' in the local championship that I still think of was in '82 — the year of the Kerry goal.

Sometimes, as that score proved, you can be the man in the right place at the right time. Ironically on a local level, Walsh Island were also going for a five-in-a-row and they beat us by two points.

I was playing corner forward in that final against them and as is often the case, when the ball wasn't coming into the full-forward line, I moved myself out to centre-forward to try to get some possession. I had hardly run out to the position when a long ball went in around the square, bobbling around the full forward line that Eugene Mulligan got to but didn't score. It was my sort of situation. Eugene was a back using his experience primarily to make scores in the forward line. I'd have fancied myself in there and regret that I moved out that 30 seconds too soon. You win some...and in our case, we went off the boil in the club after that final as we suffered a number of barren years.

As time took its toll on me, I contented myself by playing a bit of junior. In 1988, I was asked by Locky Murphy and a few others to put my name forward to train and manage Rhode, which I did. It was a natural progression and even though I was on the road as a rep a lot, I was interested enough to stand for the position. I drove down from Donegal on that Monday night to be present for the vote.

Joe Kelleghan was the club chairman that year. Paddy Kerrigan, a former Rhode player, had stepped down after posting a very impressive record as manager of Walsh Island. He sent down word that he would be interested in going forward if he was wanted.

That meant there were two people interested in the job and it was put to a vote. The result was a tie. Then someone asked if I was a member of the club. I always paid up my membership but maybe due to the increased travelling and being away a lot, I thought I was that year but when they checked, it turned out I wasn't, so I lost out as my own vote didn't count. I'm sure Walsh Island never worried that Paddy wasn't a member of their club when he was appointed and that decision by my own club upset me more than I ever let on to people.

The following Saturday night, I was at home watching television when the secretary of the Edenderry club, Tom Reilly, knocked on the door and asked if I was interested in taking over their senior team. I accepted his offer straight away and went about the job in a totally serious and professional way. We got to the county semi-final in '88 where we were beaten by Ferbane.

Even when I was Edenderry manager, I continued to play a bit of junior with Rhode. Then one evening when we played Edenderry in a game it brought home to me the madness of training one group of players and playing with another. That gave me the idea of transferring fully to Edenderry the following year.

Offaly football in 1989 was still in a pretty good state, the minors got to the All-Ireland final that year but lost to a Derry team inspired by Anthony Tohill. The year before the U-21 had won the county's only All-Ireland at that level and James Mullen, who was on that team, was picked at full-forward by us to play for Edenderry against Ferbane in Daingean in a league match.

However, on the same day his girlfriend was flying out to Australia and James wasn't around. So that posed the question to the selectors and myself: "Who will we put in?" Three of the selectors, Mickey Usher, Tony Guing and Sonny Burke said: "You should play, Seamus."

I was 38 at this stage, hadn't played senior with Rhode for a few years but knew I was sharp and fit because I was training hard under my own regime. I went with the other selectors' suggestion and picked myself to play and did fairly well against a very good club side.

Then we played the first round of the championship against Daingean — the game was fixed for... you guessed it, Rhode. My father operated the gate there for as long as I could remember and he was a sight to behold when I pulled up with a car full of Edenderry players.

I'd say it nearly killed him to let me and three other Edenderry players in at all — never mind in for free. I knew by the look of him that he was like a bag of weasels inside... but what could he do but wave us through?

That turned out to be a close encounter as we were losing by a point with a few minutes to go. I went out to centre-forward from the corner and scored two points which helped us win the game.

We then got to the semi-final where we were drawn against Rhode.

As an unbreakable custom, Daddy called into my house every Sunday morning before matches and he'd be all chat about that day's games and who would win and who would lose.

This particular morning it was different. For a start I was rushing and was conscious that I had to go down to a players' meeting. However, I wouldn't break our weekly meeting so I delayed half an hour so that we could have our cup of tea together.

For once he never mentioned football. We talked about everything under the sun, politics, local events, family issues. Anything but the elephant in the room. Then, just as we were going our separate ways outside at the gate, he turned to me and said: "I can't wish ya the best of luck today. I just hope you're not f**king killed!"

I was marked in that game by Charlie Conroy, who was a great club and county defender. We'd have marked each other countless times down the years in training and although I scored a few points off him in the first half, Charlie was also getting his fair share of clearances in. Daddy was with Paddy Smullen at the game. They were great friends and would often be together when Rhode were playing. The two of them parked on the hill during the match and anything the pair didn't call me wasn't worth recording.

Paddy had a booming voice so I could hear nearly every word he came out with while my father wasn't far behind in making himself heard. One of the things I clearly heard was the term 'traitor' hurled more than once in my direction.

In Daddy's mind, Rhode was Rhode and you couldn't beat every other team by enough. Particularly Edenderry. That was the way he was. And yet he'd be in the Hooper Farrell's house in Edenderry and they'd be great friends, he'd be in Mickey Brady's or Seán Foran's and he cherished the hours spent talking football in their company. They were the best of enemies and the best of friends, something that often happens when there is football rivalry between neighbouring people and parishes.

We were beaten by a point and needless to say, I gave Rhode a wide berth for a little while after that. I played for Edenderry that year and the following year and I was asked to stay on as manager but there was a bit of a coup in the club and I didn't want anything to do with that.

That signalled the end of the line for me in Offaly as a player but while I never foresaw it, I would play again in a final a few years later — this time in Tipperary.

PART III

CHAPTER 27

BUSINESS GOALS, OWN GOALS
(AND A SPECIAL GOAL TO END IT ALL)

I always wanted to work for myself and so at the first real opportunity, I opened a wallpaper and paint shop in Edenderry in 1976 while continuing to sell on the road. I was able to do that because Veronne ran the business during the week while I was away.

The shop was a success from the start. For the first time in our lives, it meant that when we added in my wages, we were doing really well financially. As the place got busier and busier, I left the commercial travelling altogether and threw myself full-time into the business.

We'd bought a former doctor's residence in O'Connell Square in Edenderry and were able to expand the size of the premises as well as the range we were offering. Aside from wallpaper and paint, we were now also selling tiles, tools and bits of everything really.

The business took off big time for us following the major renovation job we carried out. We had bought it in poor shape and any money we made, we ploughed it straight back into the premises. We renovated the residential part and lived there for a few years.

If there is one thing we have learned in Ireland about business, it is that as sure as there are peaks, there are troughs following closely behind. After a few good years the economy slowed in the early eighties and the recession bit. Everyone was affected by its severity.

Businesses that had given good employment in the town

began to downsize or close and as many of these were our customers, we sorely felt the knock-on effect of their lay-offs. A major blow to the community came when one of the mainstays of Edenderry for generations — the shoe factory — closed.

Many other smaller firms went belly-up too, the like of Killane Engineering where there were employees on good money, Group Textiles and even my former employers, O'Brien's Hardware, didn't survive the downturn despite having a big business reach in the town.

That was a very dark time in Ireland, so bad that the semi-states like Bord Na Móna were forced into cutbacks. No one escaped and even the companies who survived and are still in existence to this day had to prune staff and wages to survive.

Edenderry experienced closures and unemployment like every other town across the country. It differed maybe in the extent of the damage because half a dozen of its pillar employers had stopped trading — and that had a devastating effect all round.

Our shop immediately felt the pinch, and eventually we had no option but to pull down the shutters as well. That was 1984, less than two years after Offaly's All-Ireland success against Kerry.

When I closed the shop, I converted the premises into three smaller units and rented them out. We also bought a private house and turned the area where we had been living into flats. I was lucky that I had the mortgage paid off by this stage so we weren't in as bad a position as many might have felt we were.

Still, I had no option but to hit the road again — this time selling wallpaper. My employers were an English company called Morton Wall Coverings. My brief was to cover the entire 26 counties. This meant I was away a lot at a time when the kids were small.

Our daughter Naomi is our eldest and was born in 1974, then Ryan, my eldest son, came along seven years later and Shay was born a couple of weeks after the All-Ireland win in

'82. I could be away for days at a time but I tried to organise my routes whereby I got home during the week unless I was in places like Donegal or Kerry.

In my travels around the country, there was one place I really liked. I would plan it so that I could pull in, eat a bit and relax when I was on the road working. It was in Borrisokane, county Tipperary.

Having just bought the house outside of Edenderry, I had a gut instinct that I should buy this pub — the Griffin Arms — because I liked the feel of the place.

It was a lovely premises and every time I passed through there, it seemed to be doing better. It was about 60 miles from Edenderry so I knew it wouldn't make sense to drive up and down. In retrospect, very little about the place made sense if I had to dig a bit deeper, but I didn't. I went purely on my gut that it would be a good buy.

As part of that deal I had to put the property we had in Edenderry up as collateral. Once I did that, there was no bother raising the money at the time in late 1988. I had four flats and three units all paid for in Edenderry. I should have realised that this was a much better business model to stick with and if I minded what I had, I could have retired at 40.

I didn't do that, thinking that the Borrisokane investment would help build for the future for myself and the family. We took over the place and I opened it up with an inexplicable sense of optimism.

I had my suspicions within a week that it might not be quite as good as I was led to believe and within another couple of weeks I knew for certain that I'd made a huge mistake.

I'd started running the business there the week before Christmas — and I calculated that I should take in 10 grand that week — but I didn't. In fact I just about turned over three grand. If I couldn't make the business pay in the week leading up to Christmas when every pub is buzzing, I knew I was in deep trouble.

Borrisokane is a smallish place and had a population of around 1,000 when I started working in the pub there. It was a place I compared to Ferbane in Offaly in terms of size and business opportunity. I liked the place and the people and my failure there had nothing to do with them. It was all down to making a bad business decision — and one I can tell you I paid for a hundred times over.

From the day I opened it, I lost money hand over fist. Once that happens, the end is always the same — a receiver is appointed and his job is to sell what he can, for whatever he can get. There is no sentiment involved particularly for the person in the middle. I spent just a little over a year there but I ended up losing everything I had ever worked for not just in Borris ... but in Edenderry as well.

As you go through life, you hear of people losing their businesses but when it happens in such a dramatic manner as I experienced, it takes away all your confidence as a person. You have to be very strong in these dark moments to keep going — and I was.

I went up to Dublin to plead my case to the receiver. I told him I had three young kids, my wife had just had a brain haemorrhage and was trying to recover her ability to walk again. I asked him for time but also offered him every penny of the £580 a week we had coming in from the properties in Edenderry until I managed to get myself back on my feet.

Family wise, it was an even worse time as Veronne, who was only 38 then, had at one stage after the haemorrhage been given only three hours to live. I told him that story, asked him would he take the rents and when the pub was paid for, he could give me back my premises.

As I said, there was no sentiment in such a transaction and he gave me no comfort. It was a straightforward case for him — he needed to raise money immediately and refused to consider long-term options at all.

From his side, this was a black and white case; I hadn't been able to pay the bank back as I was contracted to and that was that. I was out the door.

Once he turned down my plea for a time extension to pay off the pub loan, my businesses were gone and I was back to square one. Within a short time, our Edenderry premises were put up for sale with ads being placed in the national newspapers.

At the auction in Morrissey's in Dublin there was a queue of people there to buy it. On the way in as I was climbing the stairs to the auction room, I bumped into the person who was conducting the sale.

"Will you be bidding for this place?" he asked me.

I looked him up and down, felt like telling him what I thought but decided to keep my cool. "How in the name of f**k can I bid for anything after you've taken everything that I have?" I asked.

He didn't respond to what I implied in my remark and merely said: "OK, that's alright then because if you were going to bid, we'd have needed cash or a draft as a deposit from you."

It was then that I lost control for a second and told him where to go. I still don't regret it. Before that auction date, I went around to people I knew in Edenderry who had the money to buy my property. I'm talking about businessmen like Paddy McCormack who was next door to my place and other publicans like Pat Larkin and Jimmy Mangan. The receiver was selling my property with two acres of land at the back in the square. As I expected, all of them told me not to worry, they wouldn't go near it.

Myself and my daughter, Naomi, who was 16 at the time, drove up to the auction and met up with a friend from Banagher before going in. He offered to buy the premises on my behalf. I told him that there was no point in doing that because I didn't have the wherewithal to pay him back.

When my lot came up, the auctioneer got up but could get no bid on Borrisokane; then he moved on to the property in

Edenderry. At that precise moment, I stepped up out from the crowd in the room, walked up to the front and took the mic out of his hand. I looked around the room, drew a deep breath and began talking: "Excuse me, ladies and gentlemen, my name is Seamus Darby and I am the owner of this property".

I went on to explain that Naomi had come with me and I pointed her out to the others present. I felt that my best chance to get my message across was to be honest. I explained the predicament that buying the pub in Borrisokane had placed me in with my property in Edenderry, which was about to go under the hammer.

"I bought that property that is now coming before you and paid for it and put it up as collateral for £130,000 for this bank. It is worth seven or eight times that amount," I explained.

I made it clear that as far as I was concerned, the property was not for sale. I emphasised that there was absolutely no need for the bank to sell it. I told the people at the auction that I was happy to do a deal to ensure the bank could get every penny that it was owed.

I pointed out that this could be done very easily as there was £590 a week coming in from the property and I finished by appealing to them that if they were here to buy the property, that they would desist from doing so.

With that out of the way, I handed back the mic to the auctioneer. I was now happy that I had done my very best to keep the property while outlining clearly my view that there was no reason for a sale.

There were no bids for this property either.

I took that to mean that the people there believed my sincerity was genuine. Of course, I was also aware that those wanting to sell and move on would hardly be swayed by how I had painted my predicament. I was thrilled leaving the place, though I knew the receiver was unlikely ever to come around to my point of view.

My intervention messed up the auction on the day but that

wouldn't stop other people making a bid afterwards. And that's what happened. Eventually a local person from Edenderry bought it. I never found out how much it went for as I couldn't afford to hire a solicitor to continue acting on my case. They all wanted money up front before engaging with me.

I was crestfallen when that man stepped forward and bought what we had in Edenderry but I was powerless to prevent it. I just had to let it go. For years, I was very upset but thankfully, I've moved on from there since.

In relations to the Griffin Arms in Borrisokane, it took them ages to sell it. It transpired that there never had been a seven-day licence for the place and the big pity from my point of view was that the Gardaí didn't walk in some night because that would have had to come out.

All it had was a hotel licence and even that was faulty too because it didn't have enough functioning bedrooms to qualify as a hotel. There were two little rooms with no windows that ostensibly made up the 10 bedrooms but in practice they didn't qualify as bedrooms.

These were dark, dark days. All we had worked for was now sold off and to make matters worse, my marriage too was falling apart. I had little wriggle room. The auction was in September and here I was selling wallpaper around the 26 counties on a commission basis trying to scrape a few pounds together.

It was hard-earned money. I had to sell to a hardware shop, go back to that shop a few months later and hope that I'd get paid if they had moved on some or all of my stock. More often than not that didn't happen. I could see clearly there was no present, never mind a future, in selling wallpaper at that time of recession.

I first met Noreen McGlynn in the Griffin Arms shortly after taking over there. I didn't know then that she would become a big part of my life for the following 15 years. I met her on the evening the Jimmy Magee All-Stars came to town. I played with a Tipperary selection against Jimmy's band of big names.

Normally I would line out with Jimmy's crew but this was different. I was on the other side. I loved making myself available any time I could because that All-Star set-up raised about €2.5 million over the years. Through it, I got to know a whole host of comedians and showband stars and because of it, I got to spend a memorable day one time in Las Vegas with Brendan Bowyer driving me around in his convertible.

The All-Star concept was very popular particularly in rural Ireland and as I hadn't been living long down in Tipperary, I felt it would be a great marketing opportunity for the pub. Jimmy and all the lads on his team did me a big turn by coming down to put on a show. We packed our place out that night — in fact every pub in the village was full.

Despite that stand alone successful evening, I quickly realised that the business was only ever going to fail. However, that was the night that my relationship with Noreen began. Some time earlier, Veronne and I had stopped living together.

Noreen and myself experienced some really good times as well as some bad times in our times as a couple. We lived together through the years when I managed kips of pubs in London and then came back home again when we bought the Greyhound Bar in Toomevara in 2002.

I can honestly say that in those low moments in Borris and London, I don't think I would have survived without her support. I was very attracted to Noreen from the start but it took me a while to get her to agree to go out with me. She was very decent to me and she gave me money when I hadn't a bean to keep me going.

One particular memory I have where her decency and kindness shone through was the day of the 1991 All-Ireland football final between Down and Meath. I was watching it on my own in the Griffin Arms. There wasn't a sinner in the place and I hadn't a sod of turf to put on the fire. The place was as cold as an igloo and I was totally miserable that afternoon — just nine years after the final of 1982.

Noreen brought me down a beautiful Sunday dinner and a bale of briquettes so that I could watch the match in comfort. She sat with me and we watched the game together.

It was an exciting match, Bernie Flynn kicked six points, three off either foot and Colm O'Rourke came on and despite having the flu almost led Meath to what would have been one of the most famous comebacks in history. In the end, Down held out and won by two points 1-16 to 1-14.

It was good to have something exciting going on to distract us because the business was gone down the chute. Without realising it, I had bought a lemon and there was nothing to do now but suck it up.

I knew once it went out of my hands and into the legal route, there would be nothing left in it for me. In fact, there was less than nothing as it also cost me a lot in fees trying to fight the system the best I could.

At this remove, I've long forgotten about the losses but still fondly remember Noreen's act of kindness just when I needed it most.

Borris provided me with my last competitive sporting highlight as a player. I scored a goal that I consider to be the equal if not better than the one I scored in Croke Park against Kerry. I was 31 when I scored that goal but I was 41 when I scored the other while playing for Borris in the North Tipperary Intermediate Football Final against Shannon Rovers.

The game was played in Nenagh and there was a very large and vocal crowd. As you'd expect, I was getting quite a bit of stick both from their spectators and players alike. I had been made aware in the week leading up to the match that one of their players had boasted that he wouldn't allow me steal the headlines again with a goal. During training in the lead up to the match, several of our own lads warned me to keep an eye out for danger.

And believe me, I did.

When you're playing senior football since you're 16 and had

now gone beyond 40, you know the importance of self-preservation. I had marked the hardest men in football in training like Mick O'Rourke night after night when I was fighting for my place in 1971.

Forewarned is forearmed. I could understand my opponent stating his case in advance — many often did it on the pitch as well down the years — but without realising it, he did me a favour by putting the word out. It was a close game and with 10 minutes or so to go a ball came in and I had my back to the goal. It arrived slightly too high over my head which meant I had to stretch backwards to catch it.

By over-stretching, I was wide open to a belt, so I managed to turn in mid-air and buried the ball in the net with my left — all in the one movement. I did it so quickly that I took everyone, including myself, by surprise. No opposition player got the chance to get near me, never mind lay a hand on me.

I got massive enjoyment out of that goal and even the slagging from the lads that I scored it out of fear didn't diminish the fact that execution wise, it was right up there if not slightly better than the one I got against Kerry.

CHAPTER 28
'92 — PLAYING IT AGAIN, FOR CHARITY

A few months before I decided to go to England to see if I could get back on my feet, there was a rematch and a big 'do' down in Kerry involving both teams a decade on from the '82 final. It was being played to raise money for local charities. Unfortunately, it also came at a time when my businesses had all gone and I hadn't two coppers to rub together in my pocket.

I had been short of money for quite some time and Freddie Grehan had been more than decent in looking after me. I met him in Edenderry the day before the match was due to take place on Friday, August 7. He looked surprised to see me and asked me if I was driving down in the morning to Kerry.

I told him I had no intention of going at all.

He asked me why not and I told him truthfully that I hadn't got the money to go.

He pulled out his wallet and slapped £100 into my hand. "There's no point in the rest of the team going down there if you're not there with them because it's you they'll want to see," he said.

I travelled down the following morning thanks to him and we had a great match in Tralee which ended in a draw on an unbelievable scoreline of: Offaly 5-13; Kerry's 7-7.

I scored 1-3 but Charlie Nelligan made two great saved from shots that I normally would have scored with in the first half. Then just on the stroke of half-time I drove a penalty over the bar. John Guinan was lining up to take it but there was a huge crowd that night in Tralee and they chanted my name to take it. I lashed it and I think Charlie got a hand to it, and there was a big cheer when I missed.

I must say though it was a marvellous occasion and the crowd gave us a great welcome. There was a great standard of football served up by both sides. It was a game neither side wanted to lose and in the end, it was my other great pal, Tony Maher, who had come on as a substitute, who shot over the equalising point as referee Tommy Sugrue was looking at his watch.

Kerry knew how to put on the hospitality afterwards and there was a great cheer when we heard that £1,500 was raised for the Irish Wheelchair Association and the Spinal Cord Society of Ireland.

It was a very enjoyable evening and that weekend, Wayne McCullough and Michael Carruth got their Olympic medals in Barcelona.

Freddie was right though — I had to be part of that get-together a decade later. The Kerry people were very decent and kind to me. If I had to tell them that I hadn't an arse in my trousers and was only there thanks to the generosity of a friend, I'm sure it would have been almost as big a shock to their system as the goal I scored a decade earlier.

CHAPTER 29
OFF TO A BAD START IN LONDON

My first journey to London had to be aborted before it really began in 1991. A very prominent Irishman over there promised me the sun, moon and stars in the drink business if I relocated. At the time, I was virtually penniless except for the £50 my friend Freddie slipped me as I left him at Dublin Airport.

It was lucky I had the spare cash because this man didn't show up as arranged in Ruislip GAA grounds for the Cashel King Cormacs (Tipperary) match against one of the London clubs in the All-Ireland Club quarter finals. That source of potential work totally dried up when later, he didn't return any of my calls.

I was given the name of a Roscommon man who was looking for bar staff and was told I might get a place to stay that night if I worked for him. Any port in a storm.

In England at the time, the brewery companies that owned the pubs were periodically ordered to cut back on their premises numbers over a 10-year period. What they did was look at the places that made the least money. While waiting for the guillotine to fall, they would rent out these condemned 'holdings' as they were called to get in a few extra bob. The one being offered to me fell into this category.

I met the Roscommon man and we agreed I'd do a shift in one of his other pubs that Friday and then look at the 'holding' which I could start up and run for him. The deal was that after my shift, I would make my way to this other place to stay on the Friday night. We were then due to catch up early the next morning, look at the place and see if we thought it would be feasible to get it up and running.

The closed pub was in Hackney and had no electricity when I arrived, which was well after midnight. I didn't need light to tell me I was in a kip of the highest order. I groped my way around in the dark and found a bed that you wouldn't put a dog in. It smelt like hell.

Lying down in that first night in exile, I began to cry.

I could tell by the smell of the bedclothes that I wasn't the first to lie in them since they were last washed... but I had little choice. The one decision I could make was to sleep in the clothes I was standing up in. That way I felt I was protecting myself from the surrounding filth.

In that moment, I thought again of the man who had hugged me in Croke Park and told me that I'd never see a poor day after scoring the goal in the All-Ireland final in '82. I wondered what he would have thought if he could see me. I turned my face to the damp and musty wall and sobbed myself to sleep.

Waking up to find once again that I wasn't dreaming was as disappointing in this surroundings as it was exhilarating the morning after I woke up following the Kerry game. I think Eddie Cunningham put it best in the Offaly Independent when he said: "Seamus Darby only needed to sleep on that Sunday night...there was no need to dream because they had all come true out on that pitch earlier that day."

Now it wasn't a case of dreams but my worst nightmares.

I got up, went downstairs and surveyed the cut of the place. It was a bombsite. I would normally have turned on my heels and walked away. But beggars can't be choosers. The Roscommon man said he would come over early but didn't. To pass the time, I began tidying the pub up. There was no food at all in the place. I had very little money left from the cash I got from Freddie — just change in my pocket.

I was hoping this individual would turn up, pay me for the shift I'd worked the previous day and then strike a bargain over the place I was now in. I worked hard all morning hoping to impress but by lunch time there was still no sign of him.

Ireland were playing England in rugby that day and I decided around half two to go into the nearest pub and watch the game.

When I checked my pockets, I saw that I had the price of a bottle of 7-Up and a packet of crisps. That would have to be my breakfast and dinner and probably my supper as well on this first London Saturday.

Normally, I love watching sport but I was preoccupied with my own thoughts and wondering would this man show up at all that day?

As I was watching the second half of the game, my attention was drawn to someone coming in my direction — it was the Roscommon man. We hadn't hit it off that well the previous day when I first met him and I could tell from his demeanour now that he was aggressive and feeling hard done by. He walked straight up in front of my eye-line, blocking the television screen and stood over me like a headmaster looking down on a schoolboy: "What do you think you're doing?"

I looked at him with a feeling of both despair and anger inside but answered in a quiet tone: "I'm watching the match."

He said: "Are you not supposed to be above sorting out the pub?"

I replied: "I did that all morning right up to about an hour ago. When you didn't show up by then, I decided to come up here for a mineral and to watch a bit of the rugby."

That was totally true, but it didn't allay the agitation in his demeanour. He shook his head.

"I don't think this is going to work out between us?" he stated irritably in a manner that left me little choice but to agree.

"If that's your attitude, I'd say you're right," I said, again without raising my voice.

He made a beeline for the door.

I called after him: "Hang on a second."

He looked at me, probably expecting me to beg for the job.

"You might want these," I said.

I threw the keys of the pub, which he had forgotten he gave me the previous day, in his direction. He tried to catch them but they spilled onto the floor. He picked them up, turned away and disappeared out the door.

I had hoped that the final exchange would see him put his hand in his pocket and give me the money he owed me. In reality, I knew this guy was a mean bastard and that was the last thing on his mind.

I should have asked him straight out for what he owed me before handing back the keys, but that wasn't and isn't my style. My pride wouldn't let me do it.

I ended up watching the rest of the match in a daze. When the game ended I knew Ireland had lost by 38-9 on that first day of Spring 1992. I knew I had lost too and I wasn't sure if I could recover. As I walked out on to the high street, all I could remember thinking was: "What am I going to do now?"

Here I am in London with no money in my pocket and if I'm honest, I'm not even sure where I am in the city. Aside from a few pence in change in my pocket, the only thing I had with me was a chequebook. I walked down into the nearest tube station I could find and approached the person in the ticket office knowing I was backing a long shot — praying that she might cash a cheque for me.

As I explained in the foreword earlier, that woman in the booth did me a massive favour that day. She cashed the cheque for someone who had slept in their clothes and hadn't a banker's card to back up the cheque he was trying to get changed. By way of explanation, all I can genuinely think is that someone, somewhere must have been praying for me.

I recall this incident mindful that if someone walked into my pub tonight and asked the same of me, I'd be very reluctant to do what that person did for me. Although I had no money on me, I did have a few pounds left in the bank account and the cheque didn't bounce. At least I didn't have to feel guilty that I betrayed the lady's trust.

I shudder to think where I would have gone if I hadn't been given the price of a tube ticket and a few pounds change to get me to a friend of a friend who had agreed to give me a roof over my head for a few nights. It was one of the lowest times in my life but luckily had a happy ending of sorts.

I got to the flat and was happy to have a base for a few days. However, I knew I'd have to abort my mission by returning home again after I got a loan to cover my travel back. When I got back to Ireland, I tried to find work locally but failed. In desperation, I began selling sweets wholesale to shops. It kept me busy and brought in a few bob to keep me going. But long-term I had commitments to family and banks and I needed to earn a lot more money than that business could ever pay.

This was a time when my confidence was totally shot. The business had gone and on the personal front, Noreen was staying in Ireland and I was about to leave my family behind and head back to England.

I finally got a job there thanks to a really lovely man from Wexford named Phil Duggan. He worked for Saxon Inns, which was owned by a man from Northern Ireland. At the time they had about 15 pubs in their stable.

One Sunday night while I was still in Ireland, I was flicking through the Sunday World newspaper and I saw an advertisement looking for a barman in London. It is hard for people to realise how impossible it was for a guy like me to get a proper job in Ireland at the time. Having seen the job, I was so desperate that I rang the number in the small ad that Sunday night.

Luckily it was answered immediately. The person on the other end of the line asked me where I was from.

I said: "Offaly".

He then asked me my name.

"Seamus Darby," I replied.

"Are you the footballer?"

When I said I was, we talked football for a good while and then like the nice guy he is, he said to me confidentially: "Seamus, I wouldn't offer you this job because it's not a great place and the money isn't that good either."

I asked him if there was a place to stay going with the bar job.

He said there was.

"Right," I said, "I'll take it."

This was the early nineties and my level of pay was only £147 a week. It was money and I had no choice but to take it. My last official job working in Ireland as a rep for Morton Wall Coverings wasn't paying because people had no money to buy such luxuries as wall coverings.

Going to England wasn't an ideal alternative but it was my only way out. I went over to Chalk Farm in London near Camden Town to work in the Fiddler's Elbow pub. I was very lucky. Phil and myself hit it off from the moment we began speaking on the telephone. He was a great GAA man and as decent a person as ever stood in shoe leather.

Unlike the previous encounters in London, I knew this guy would look out for me. In fact, he promised that the first pub manager's job that came up with his company would be earmarked for me. That gave me a great lift and made it easier in those early days and weeks away from home. The chance of a quick promotion in any job is a good driver.

It was hard relocating as Noreen and I had just got together a short-time before that. In Edenderry, Veronne was far from well; she had been close to dying and was now having to mind three kids, the youngest, Shay, was only nine at the time. She was on social welfare but I promised her I would send her home as much as I could to help her through. And I did.

I never told Veronne straight out that I was involved with Noreen but she knew and I knew she knew. I don't think she was terribly surprised. Naturally, there was a certain tension between us for a time but we got through it in our own way.

The first thing I had to do for everyone was earn enough money — going to Chalk Farm was the first step in doing that.

I flew over for fifty quid on a one-way ticket and unlike others who promised to meet me before, Phil was kind enough to pick me up at the airport. I'd asked him how I'd recognise him and he quipped: "I'll be the biggest and ugliest person there."

That was Phil. Full of good humour. He was a big man alright but he was a good one too. He certainly looked after me and I'll always be grateful to him for that. He was from around Rosslare Strand in Wexford and now lives in Camross in Laois.

We arrived into the pub on a Tuesday night and he asked me if I'd have a drink with him. We had a pint of cider apiece and then I was shown my sleeping quarters. You couldn't swing a cat in it, but I wasn't complaining. I'd never lived in a city in my life and now all I could hear outside were police cars, lorries and buses screeching to a halt and people shouting. It took me weeks to get used to sleeping in those conditions.

The person running the pub was Peter Woods. Officially, he was the manager but his big interest was traditional Irish music. He also loved to write stories and was forever reading. It was mostly an Irish clientele but others came in there too. I worked as a barman for about six months and enjoyed it because these were the best of characters I had around me as colleagues.

True to his word, Phil called me one day and said a manager's job had become vacant in The Old Farm House in Kentish town. He offered me the job and I was delighted to take it. Straight away I doubled my money — I was now earning £300 a week.

The Fiddler's Elbow had taught me a lot in a short time — and I applied it in my new station. I was only really settling in at the new place when he offered me even more money to take over the Brewery Tap in Barking about six months later.

How could I say no when Phil said there was another £100 a week going with this post. He knew I had commitments at home and was trying to ensure I had enough to send back and also have spending money for myself. However, he did warn me that I was taking over a rough pub in a rough district of East London and there was a chance it mightn't work out.

As is often the case, money talked. To survive financially before I left Ireland to start the pub circuit in London, I went into the bank and got an agreement to suspend my mortgage repayments. Now with the new level of earnings I was on, I was able to recommence payments on the home house. I felt an incredible sense of achievement in being able to do that.

I went out to Barking aware that this pub and clientele would be no bed of roses. In truth though, I didn't foresee how dangerous my short time there would turn out to be. Fortunately, just before I'd left the Old Farm House, a friend of mine, Mike McGuinness from Edenderry, rang up asking if I would put him up if he came to London and maybe give him a start with a few shifts.

He too had faced tough times like myself due to his involvement in a pub. I told him to come over and he could stay with me for as long as he liked. Mike found himself work in various pubs around the city and then when I went to Barking, he came to work there as well. It was to prove a real eye-opener for both of us, having to deal with situations that sometimes looked even more dangerous than you'd see in television dramas or in Eastenders.

The tipping point came when a woman began to openly sell drugs in the pub. I knew this could be a really unpleasant moment but I had to put a stop to that. What I didn't factor in was that she was an ex-girlfriend of one of the Kray twins, which probably explained her sense of entitlement to do whatever she wanted on the premises.

In hindsight, I might have been a bit more circumspect than I was. I took the blunt approach and simply ordered her out of the pub and told her she was barred from ever coming back.

She had some sort of dalliance with an old geezer from Dublin who was living off her ill-gotten gains. A huge row flared and I was thankful that a young Westmeath lad I had working in the place was there to back me up that evening. As half the pub attacked us, I shouted to him: "Get out the bats!" We had two baseball bats behind the counter. I'm telling you, we needed both of them that night.

We 'bet' the crap out of anybody who moved and I was lucky myself that I didn't end up dead or at best badly injured. While I was swinging the bat, luckily I managed to see in the corner of my eye a fella coming from behind me with a stool aimed at my head. I jumped out of the way and took the full force on my back instead of my head. It was a fierce blow but it was better to take the hit there as he would certainly have cracked my skull. We finally cleared the place of people but the old pub looked like a bomb had hit it.

I got up the next morning, feeling fairly sore, cleaned up the place and got it ready for the next shift at 3pm. I was looking forward to a break and I was happy that I was leaving it in the competent hands of Mike.

I went upstairs, put my feet up and was looking forward to an afternoon nap. I was no more than 20 minutes there when the old Dublin guy walked in below with a gun in his hand — wild west-style — demanding my whereabouts. He told Mike he was going to kill me for what I did to his girlfriend the previous night.

I could hear the commotion and knew that potentially this fella meant business. I've no doubt if I had been down in the bar that afternoon, he was in such an agitated state that he would have shot me.

Mike talked him out of his rage, telling him to put the gun away and have a pint. He told him I was only in for a short time and wouldn't be around again. When my would-be assassin left the premises, I went down and thanked Mike for saving my bacon.

I then telephoned Phil.

I told him he wasn't exaggerating when he said it was a rough joint. When I reported what had just occurred, his advice was: "Seamus, we've got to get you out of there quickly."

Once again I was back to square one. I rang Noreen, told her the story and she agreed with Phil that I should get out. She suggested that the best thing would be to come home for a week or two, let the dust settle and then see if Phil could find something better well away from that den of inequity.

My return coincided with the time Noreen was on her annual holidays from Proctor and Gamble where she worked as a supervisor. While back in Ireland, she told me she had made her mind up that she was going to go back with me to London. I explained that I couldn't really make a commitment with the way things were financially up in the air once more. I didn't have a job and I also didn't want to take the responsibility of allowing her give up her really good staff job.

However, she was adamant. She said her mind was made up and she was going no matter what I said. I suppose at the end of the day that decision was hers and hers alone to make.

We got the bus from Nenagh in Tipperary to London and I was really shocked that she would give up such a good position to take a chance in England with me. I promised myself that if she was making a commitment like that, I would give it everything and try to give the relationship a real go. I pledged to work hard at my job (when I got one) and also work hard at the relationship.

When we arrived in London, I rang Phil. He said he had nothing immediately available but informed us that we could stay in a big apartment over the HQ of the Saxon Inns for as long as we wanted. That was a real plus given that Noreen was now with me. While I was hanging around waiting for a pub to crop up, through Phil I met a Romanian man named Spiro Titus, who was a likeable sort though I never could fathom him totally.

He offered me this pub he had on his books for a pittance.

He was the area manager for a massive brewery and he gave me this holding — The Prince Regent — that truly was one of the worst kept places I'd ever seen. It was located on Orb Road, near the East Street.

I wore two scrubbing brushes out trying to take the dirt out of the carpet that was embedded in the pub. I was on my knees for two weeks non-stop doing it. I didn't have any real alternative as I'd no money to buy new stuff. While it was never going to be the best place or best pub, I put a lot of effort into making it a friendly 'local' to have a drink in and we spent six or seven years there — and ended up enjoying the experience.

I started making money. We kept a few lodgers and I worked in the pub for every hour that it demanded, even if it sometimes meant going right through the night. For the first time in a long time, I was able to live, pay my mortgage at home and save up enough to go on a holiday.

I knew though that because this was a holding pub, I was on borrowed time from day one. The surprising thing was it lasted so long. Then one day without any prior warning, it was sold from under our feet.

I then switched to the Red Lion on Walworth Road, near the Elephant and Castle district and I ran that for a Meath man for about a year. It too was one of the brewery's worst pubs and in its turn it was sold on. For the record, it is now a block of flats.

After leaving this place, Noreen applied for and was given approval for a council apartment. She also got a job managing a pub. I switched over to yet another pub called 'The Gowlett' in East Dulwich but it didn't take long to realise that this wasn't working out.

I changed tack totally then and went working with a Kerry company called Murphys, who looked after the upkeep of railways in England.

As Kerry lads, they never held anything against me on the football front and I was delighted to work for them for three years. They made you earn your keep but I never had a problem with that. It was physical work and considering my background as a young lad, that was no problem to me. I was carrying sleepers, taking out rails for laying and carrying cables up and down the lines around London. This sort of labour also kept me in shape and as I'd be inclined to put on a bit of weight, it was a perfect workout. Part of my job was to walk the lines, I'd say I lost about a stone and a half weight in my time with them. Like Glen Campbell, I was a lineman for the county — though in my case, I wasn't too sure what county it was.

There was also better pay in this line of work plus the fact that I wasn't there until one o'clock in the morning as would have been the case in the pub business. The downside was they'd be looking for you to work weekends as well, such was the demand to keep lines open.

I managed to overlap some of the time on the railways with running pubs at night, but I knew I could only keep that going for a short time. It helped get money together, which was why I'd gone to London in the first place.

I parted with Murphys on friendly terms because they wanted to promote me and send me down to oversee work they had got a contract for in Southampton. That would have meant living down there and I had no intention of relocating again now that Noreen and I had a place.

The White Horse in the White City area of London was the pub that nearly undid all the good work. I'd taken over the place and was trying to build up business so that it might in time become a nice little earner, as they say. Around that time, I got urgent word that my mother was in a bad way and close to death. Stephen and Eileen phoned advising me to get home as quickly as possible.

Under normal circumstances, I would have put off going home until the following week because I had put virtually every penny into an upcoming event in the pub by buying in a huge amount of drink stock, plus food and cigarettes.

Noreen rightly said it was a big risk if I wasn't in the pub all that weekend, but the message was clear and I wanted to see Mammy alive one more time.

I decided to hire more staff for the few days so that I could go straight away. I got the last flight available out of London and hired a car in Dublin Airport where I met up with my daughter, Naomi.

We drove down to Rhode as fast as we could, hoping we'd get there before she died. I remember when we pulled up outside the house, Kevin Farrell was there waiting.

"Run quickly before she's gone," he said, opening the door to help me out of the car.

Naomi and I got there in time before my mother drew her last breath. It was a mad dash but it was lovely to be able to hold her hand before she died and to tell her how much I loved her for all she had done for me.

The following Tuesday evening, the day of her burial, I bought everyone in Doyle's pub in Rhode a drink in her honour. This wasn't an attempt to show off that I was doing well in London or anything like that; it was simply that I felt I owed Mammy one final salute for all she had done for me and the rest of the family.

I loved my mother in a special way because she 'got' me. And she looked out for me, even if I was in the wrong. Like the time Catch Grennan, John Kavanagh and myself got fond of mitching from school. I was a bit reluctant at first but once I started it, I found it hard to go into class at all. On one particular week, we stayed away three days on the trot along the canal bank, lying out in the good weather and passing the time playing games. Myself and the lads knew it was important to go in to the school for part of the week and had planned to attend the following day.

However, Daddy got a loan of a tractor of Cotton's farm to draw in the potatoes and said he needed me to give him a hand. "There'll be no problems because you haven't missed a day all year," he said innocently.

What could I do? The two of us got up early the following

morning and went at it hammer and tongs. Around midday as we were driving another load around to the back of the house, I was struck with panic when I saw the Principal of the Tech, Con Sullivan, pulling up at our door in his car. My mother came outside to talk to him.

We put the load into the shed and after I heard Con's car drive away a few minutes later, I went round and as casually as I could said: "What did he want, Mammy?"

"You," she said.

"You haven't been in school the last three days and he was looking to see how you were."

"And what did you tell him?"

"I said you'd been drawing in potatoes the last four days with your father," she said, looking at me with a wry smile on her face.

That was Mammy, she'd let me know I wasn't fooling her but she'd never let me down.

Her death was a really sad time for us — we were all distraught. I knew it would hit Daddy hard later that week when everyone who had been around for the funeral had gone. I'd love to have been able to stay on to help him over that time but I had to get back to my business as soon as I could.

I returned to London on the Wednesday in low spirits — and then got hit with something that financially knocked me for six.

When I pulled up at the White Horse premises to check on how the weekend party had gone, I was greeted by the sight of a lock and chain on the front door of my premises. I forced my way in to find that everything had been cleared out.

I'd been taken to the cleaners while I was at home.

When I called the nearest police station to report the theft, they were already aware of the robbery. They told me they visited the pub in the early hours of the previous Sunday morning but by that time, all the stock had disappeared.

It looked like I would have to start all over again because

I knew the prospect of getting paid out on insurance was nil. The theft was an inside job and those in charge took advantage of my absence to get a van to the door where they loaded up anything that wasn't nailed down. The drink and cigarettes were the big attraction — I lost thousands of pounds in stock and having spent whatever extra few bob I had, it meant I was on my uppers once more.

I was feeling very sorry for myself — no pub, no job, no money and my head was all over the place at the loss of my mother.

I walked around in a trance for days. I wondered what in God's name I was going to do. For a second time a pub had cleaned me out and I wondered should I continue in this field or do something like drive a taxi where at least your hours would be at your own discretion.

In the week following the heist I hadn't anything to do but mope around the flat. I went out to get milk and picked up a London Evening Standard to see if there were jobs going. There weren't.

The following morning Noreen and I were having our breakfast when the post arrived. There was one letter delivered with my name on it. It was from one of the banks where I had an account.

The letter explained that I now qualified for a loan of £15,000 after being a customer for so many years. Those letters normally suck you in by offering all kinds but once you get in touch, there is a catch somewhere.

Having nothing better to do, I said to Noreen that I'd walk up to the nearby branch of the bank and check out what really was on offer. It was only about five minutes away.

When I went in, I was served by a lovely young woman of Irish parentage. I told her about the letter I had received in the post. She was very friendly and we got to talk about where I was from and from what part of Ireland her own family came. She said she was just back from a weekend in Cork and was still recovering from it.

She sat down at her desk, talking all the while as she worked. Then — and I'm not exaggerating here — she looked across the counter to me and said: "That money is now in your account, Seamus."

She gave me some documents to sign saying I had taken out a loan of £15,000 as well as the usual terms of repayment. I couldn't believe it. Then a little light went on in my head — this has to be my mother helping me back up on my feet again.

I was very close to her all my life; we had the same sense of humour and she always looked out for me while she was alive. Now in death she had come to my aid and the strange thing is that from that day to this, I've had some financial challenges to overcome but I have never worried about money again.

CHAPTER 30

BOB GELDOF — I DON'T LIKE MOANERS

I've had a fair few regrets between one thing and another but my biggest in terms of day-to-day living is not throwing Bob Geldof out of my car in London in 2001.

I was fed up with the long hours in pubs so I thought I'd try my hand in the taxi business after once again seeing an ad in the local paper looking for drivers. I went up to the taxi company where they installed a metre and a radio and sent me out to work. Obviously I didn't know London any way well and there was no Google maps at that time, but as is the case in many jobs, much of it is about having a good map and learning by your mistakes.

I was about a week at the taxi game when one day I knew I had to take Noreen to Heathrow Airport as she was going home to Ireland. I rang in ahead to the taxi radio, told them I'd be available if they had any work from the airport.

They checked up and came back over the radio saying that I was to pick up a Mr Bob Geldof, with another person, who were both flying in from Dublin.

The plane was due to land at 12.15 and I recognised him immediately as he made his way out onto the concourse. I had written up his name and when he saw it, he walked over to where I was.

He had his two hands in his pockets and he just looked at me without actually speaking. I'd have known enough about Bob from his time with the Boomtown Rats and appearances on the Late, Late Show on RTE to realise he wouldn't be in Croke Park every Sunday. In fact, I'd say he had little or no interest in

Gaelic football. I had no expectations for him to recognise me as a footballer or as someone who scored that goal but I was satisfied that from the cut of me, he knew I was from Ireland.

In those circumstances, people often ask what part of the country you're from etc, but in Bob's case, there was no small talk. Absolutely none.

He checked the time and said: "I need to be in Knightsbridge by one o'clock." That was giving me a very short time to negotiate the traffic in London and arrive by his desired time. I knew it was 10 or 12 miles and I also knew you wouldn't do that time on a broomstick. I told him that it was a big ask but stressed that I'd get him there as quickly as I could.

I then noticed this very nice woman coming in our direction pulling two suitcases with a bag on each shoulder. Jeanne Marine, later to become his wife, was his girlfriend at the time and she stopped beside the car. Immediately I took the luggage and put it in the boot while opening the door to allow her sit in the back seat of the car.

When we were underway driving, Bob mentioned a particular hotel and asked me if I knew where it was. I told him truthfully that I didn't but would get him to Knightsbridge and he might have to guide me to it when we got into the area.

I never forgot what he said and more importantly the demeaning way he said it.

"Oh for f**k's sake, Irish drivers, you're all the same."

My biggest regret is I didn't jump on the brakes there and then and say: "Get the f**k out."

I should have done that to preserve my own dignity but his partner had been so nice when I helped her get the stuff into the car that I couldn't insult her in that way.

Geldof never spoke a word for the rest of the journey as fortunately I spotted the hotel he was looking for as I was driving down near Harrods.

When I pulled up, he jumped out without saying anything and just stormed off. Jeanne got out and apologised profusely.

She then said that the luggage would have to be transported to Battersea as they were attending a function but would be out there later.

Now Battersea was another few miles south across the river and I had no idea where it was but again I had to find my way there. She asked if I could get there before two o'clock as she had someone in the place they would be staying to take in the luggage if I got there by then. As it happened, traffic was very heavy and it was nearer to three before I pulled up.

By that stage, there was no response at the address I was given so I rang back into the taxi company to see if they could tell me what to do next. They checked with the phone number they got when the original booking was made and rang me back to say I would have to return the cases and bag to the reception at the hotel and say they were for Bob Geldof.

I found it hard enough driving out but now it was rush hour and I'd forgotten the way so it took me a few hours to get back into Knightsbridge and deposit the stuff at the hotel reception.

Finally, I got home at 7pm totally exhausted. I rang in to the taxi firm to tell them I was now off duty and asked when and how much I could expect from the six hours work for Mr Geldof. They said he had an account and that I would get £17 for that particular job — but it wouldn't be paid for a month.

That finished my taxi days. I would have spent the £17 on petrol. I jumped into the car and pulled up at the taxi HQ later that evening, told them to take their radio and other stuff out of it and explained that I wouldn't be working for them again. Bob Geldof had finished my career as a taxi driver.

Looking back on that incident now, I often wonder why I got so annoyed over it. It had nothing to do with anything other than one Paddy not recognising another and at least giving him the time of day. That's the long and short of it. I admired Bob for what he did in Africa but I have no time for the way he treated me that day. And that's why that particular incident rankles with me still.

I was shocked and hurt but at my age, I was used to life's ups and downs and knew the best thing to do for both of us would be to get our affairs sorted legally.

CHAPTER 31

HOME — WHERE
THE HEART IS

All the while I was in England, there was always the hankering to go back to Ireland. One day I was reading an Irish newspaper and I saw there was a pub — The Greyhound Bar — for sale in Toomevara. Noreen had mentioned it to me a few days earlier but I didn't think too much about it. I felt that with my previous experience in the trade in Ireland and after years going around London into pubs of various standards that I wanted out of that business. I was 51 at the time and was hoping for a bit more quality time.

Noreen though was keen to buy it but I wasn't sure about the venture, though I now wanted to live back in Ireland. A short time later we were home on holidays and myself and Noreen's brother-in-law drove over one Thursday night and had a few pints in the bar.

The place was hopping.

The following Saturday I drove back and talked to the owner, John Fitzpatrick. I asked him if it was sold and he explained that a man had put a bid on it but there was no deposit paid.

Pubs were flying in Ireland at the time and I knew I would have to go into serious debt to get it.

I told John that if the man he was talking to bought it, that was fine. I asked him to let me know if for some reason, the deal fell through. I left him my mobile number in case he needed to get in touch. If there was a hitch I told him I would buy the pub at the price he had agreed with the other person — provided I could raise the money.

Within a week of my return, John rang to inform me that the other man had pulled out and the pub was mine if I wanted it.

It took a while but eventually I got the money from the ACC in Dublin. I had to go over and back six weeks in a row but at the end of it all, I got the finances in place. There were no concerns over my previous Irish pub experience as that was with another bank, the ICC. Besides, it had been 12 years since that had happened and no one was out of pocket — certainly not the banks or legal people — except myself. I was the one who lost all the money in that transaction.

It was a great feeling to be returning to Ireland and the fact that we would now have our own business was a bonus. We moved in straight away and lived over the premises for three or four years. The pub was very busy in this period but unfortunately, it was around then that Noreen told me she had met someone else.

At that time, 2007, we had been together for over 15 years so I'd be lying if I didn't admit that it was a big shock to my system. What was worse was that I hadn't seen it coming.

I was shocked and hurt but at my age, I was used to life's ups and downs and knew the best thing to do for both of us would be to get our affairs sorted legally.

I got onto an auctioneer company, James Young in Dublin, and asked that they put the pub up for sale. The cost of that alone was hefty but it had to be done.

Unfortunately but not unexpectedly given the timing in the cycle of the Celtic Tiger, there were no bids at the auction.

Youngs put a value on the pub that meant we still owed half that figure. In that circumstance, the best thing was for one of us to buy the other out.

Noreen agreed with that assessment and I thought it probably would be better if she bought it as she was from Toomevara. I assured her that I would be happy to move on if that was the case.

Later that year, it became a lot more difficult to raise money because of the massive downturn in the economy. Noreen then informed me that she was having no success with the banks in raising money. It was then up to me to try. I rang a manager

— a good pal in ACC — who I knew was a decent person and a mad GAA man. I told him the story and he asked me to leave it with him, saying he would ring me back within a week or so.

It was early December and Noreen had indicated she was going to Scotland that Christmas. I resolved that I wasn't going to work myself to the bone for nothing over the holidays, given the situation the pub was now in.

When the bank manager rang me back, he said he was finding it hard to raise the money. He explained how financially everything had gone very quiet. He said the top man in the organisation was from a great GAA family and he organised a meeting with him within the week.

The three of us sat down together and I was frank and to the point. I told them Noreen was going to Scotland; it was coming up to Christmas and I wasn't going to strangle myself working over the holiday period for nothing.

"I'm going to be very straight with you," I told them, "if I don't get the money, I will be working in New York by Christmas — it's as simple as that. If you tell me now there's no money in it for me, I'll give you lads the keys and walk away."

I could tell they were shocked, but they also saw that I meant what I said. They asked me to leave it with them for a day or two — and I did. I drove back to Edenderry and stayed the night with Freddie. We went out and had a right few pints. Freddie knew my story with Noreen and the banks better than anyone. He was a great sounding board to have — if only to let off steam.

Driving through Daingean two days later, the phone rang. It was exactly two weeks before Christmas and the bank manager had an answer. He told me they would loan me the money but I wouldn't have it until after Christmas.

I'm sure he had moved mountains on my behalf to get the deal through but I dug my heels in — either I had the money so that I could buy Noreen out of the business or I'd be in New York for Christmas.

He pointed out the tight timeline and the fact that it was near Christmas made it impossible to get the finances in place any quicker. I stuck to my guns and said I either get the money immediately or it was curtains.

I must have wrecked the poor man's head but once again he came up trumps for me. He arranged it so that the day before Christmas Eve I could go to the ACC in Dublin, collect my cheque, bring it to my solicitor and also have Noreen present for signing documents etc.

Noreen didn't really want to be there but I said to her: "Noreen, you are going to get a big cheque which is waiting for you and if I was you, I would come over and collect it."

She agreed, accompanied me to the various places and signed off on the place. The solicitor took the cheque off me and then I wrote one for Noreen and actually lodged it in the bank for her that Christmas Eve morning. It would be too glib to say she got a great Christmas present because this was a difficult time for both of us.

It was very emotional, particularly that morning. She began to cry and said she was sorry the way things turned out. I was genuinely sorry too it had come to this but I had to accept that she wanted to move on.

I was now back in big debt due to the changed circumstances surrounding ownership of the pub. Not for the first time, I knew the years ahead would be difficult. Jobs were being lost again left, right and centre and the pub trade had taken a hammering across the country. My turnover reduced by nearly two-thirds of what it had been in the good times. If that wasn't bad enough, I now had a new mortgage to pay back as well.

It was tough trying to keep the ship afloat financially... but despite a few scary moments, I could see light at the end of the tunnel. Not too many people were aware of how tight things were for me — only a few very, very close friends — who I knew had my back in my darkest days.

CHAPTER 32

FIGHTING A NEW FOE — CANCER

I was 63 years old when I found out I had cancer. I had no symptoms and at no time leading up to the diagnosis was I feeling unwell or anything like that.

A number of years earlier while living in London I got into the routine of having a medical every year and it was because of this good habit that the cancer was discovered. My partner of that time, Noreen, was fastidious in checking her health and made sure I followed her example. It is a habit that I am glad I took up because without such checks, I might have not caught it in time.

I got my blood tested by Dr Jarlath Healy, a Wexford native, who has his practice in Toomevara. When I went back for the results, he said there was a trace of blood in my urine, which although not visible, was detected in the test.

Like all good doctors, he didn't want to alarm me but recommended that I get it checked out. He mentioned that the symptom could be a sign of something else and the best thing was to go to a consultant urologist, Garett Durkan, in Galway.

In those moments you pick up signs and I was a bit concerned when I saw he was worried there might be complications. A biopsy was carried out and when I went to see Garrett a few weeks later as we had arranged, he sat me down and then told me straight out that I had cancer.

I was finding it hard to concentrate when I heard that but he brought me back by the matter-of-fact, gentle way he explained what I could do to beat it.

He said there were three possibilities for me to consider:

1. Have an operation

2. Have chemo and hopefully that would keep it at bay or

3. Do nothing at all — but I would die if I chose that route.

Naturally, I agreed that the third one wasn't a real option. It was then a question of going for the one that offered me the better chance in the two remaining options.

I though about it for a minute and asked him as the expert what he himself would be inclined to do if he were in my situation?

He didn't answer me directly at that time. Instead he said: "Seamus, I'm the surgeon who will be operating on you. Let me fix up a meeting with the people who will be looking after the chemo end. I would like you to talk to them and after that, you can make up your own mind".

When I met the medical personnel as he had suggested, they explained the different routes I could take and the effects each would have on my quality of life in the future. They pointed out that if I had the operation and the cancer returned, it would then be possible to have the chemo but if you have the chemo first and the cancer came back, then it would not be possible to have the operation.

Once I heard that, it was a no-brainer — it had to be the operation. I went into the Galway Clinic in June, 2015 and was thankful that my routine of regular medical visits had given me the best chance of survival and recovery.

Men in particular are not very good at going to their doctor when they are not feeling well or discover something. I think Irish men have always hoped these things will go away if they ignore them.

I've always encouraged lads visiting my pubs in England and Ireland to go for annual visits to their doctors simply because it makes sense. If you have nothing, you get the all clear and if you have something, well you are catching it a lot earlier than if you wait for the symptoms to develop beyond the point where in some cases, you cannot be helped.

It makes total sense and I'd appeal to men of my own age or even younger to go for a check-up this week if they haven't ever had one. Doctors call prostate cancer 'the silent killer', and it's also a major cause of men's deaths in later life.

As of now — the summer of 2019 — it is a case of so far so good for me. I feel genuinely blessed to have caught it early and to have recovered. I appreciate that I am one of the lucky ones, and I'm thankful to God for that.

After the operation I asked the surgeon how he thought things had gone and Garrett said: "I think I got it all". Even better from my point of view was the fact that I didn't have to have chemotherapy as is normally the case. That was four years ago.

When you hear the word 'cancer' from a medical person, it puts many things in perspective and also gets you thinking about where you stand on issues. For people my age, the reflex reaction to such news is to pray — that's if you still believe in God.

I was brought up a Catholic and like many others, a lot of what I was taught no longer makes sense in the present day. Religion doesn't have the hold over Irish people that it had in my parents' time.

People are more a la carte about it and have dispensed with much of the negativity such as sins and guilts being handed out like confetti.

Personally, I don't attend Mass that often but when I go, I get a real lift out of the experience. I'd have gone regularly until I got into the pub business. Even now, if I get the chance, I like to slip into Nenagh, which has a big church where no one knows me, and attend noon mass on a Sunday.

I also like to pray but maybe not in a conventional way. If I'm alone, whether at home or maybe when driving along in the car, I'd think of people dead and gone as well as those still alive and wish them well.

That word 'cancer' frightens people and it certainly floored me.

My whole life came up before my eyes in that instant. I wondered if it meant the end. As I said elsewhere, I have often had bad news in life and in business and I'm blessed with a disposition that tries to focus on being positive.

Cancer made me realise there was nothing I could do. I was powerless. You go from walking into a doctor's surgery thinking about what's going on in your life and what you think is important. You walk out the same door half an hour later and you're wondering will there be a life there at all for much longer?

That is a big change in a few short minutes. I suppose that is where your religious background comes in because you turn to God or the higher being in your life and you ask for help.

We never told Daddy; by that stage he was in a nursing home. Fortunately he still had his full faculties but we didn't want to bother him because he was 93 years old.

Since my mother died, it's become something of a ritual for me to talk to her about my problems. Having that outlet is very important to me. With the cancer, I knew she wouldn't let me down if it were at all possible.

She didn't.

As well as my mother, I'd often pray to my granny or Fr. McWey for help in times of trouble. Ever since my friend and brother-in-law, Kevin Farrell died, I talk to him too when I'm looking for clarity on things in my life.

The cancer incident wasn't the first time I'd had health issues.

About seven years before and totally out of the blue one day, I lost the sight in one eye. I was driving up home on the road between Kilcormac and Tullamore when it happened.

I went immediately to my own doctor and was then referred to see Mr Phillip Reilly, a Consultant Ophthalmic surgeon in Limerick. He examined me and said I'd had a mini-stroke, claiming that I was lucky I got it in the back of my eye. He explained that it was like a pipe with a weakness in it that explodes.

He said he would treat me by administering three injections into the pupil of my eye. If for some reason they didn't work, he would then give me three more.

However, if the second bout didn't work then I'd lose the sight in that eye. I was fortunate in this instance too as I got my sight back with his first course of treatment.

Since then and as a way of showing my gratitude for the success of my own case, I am happy to lend my name and do a number of walks for Fighting Blindness.

*It is said almost categorically
at this stage by the public,
fed on whispers and rumours
down the years, that drink was
at the root of my downfall.*

CHAPTER 33

DRINK — THE RUMOURS AND THE REALITY

One of the main reasons I decided to write this book is to clear up even to a small degree some perceptions that have stalked the public highways down the decades since the 1982 All-Ireland Final.

If I got a penny for every time people spoke of my drink problem either behind my back or to my face, I could shut up shop and retire without any financial worries, even if I live to be a hundred.

It is said almost categorically at this stage by the public, fed on whispers and rumours down the years, that drink was at the root of my downfall. People equate the serious business problems I encountered down the years with my so-called drinking problem.

The fact that this persists was confirmed by a friend as late as June gone by when a person on being told about this book, asked: "Does he go into his drink problem in it?"

There are variations as to how I got this problem with some stories saying that since I was a young lad, I've liked the sauce. The real rumours, however, centre on what happened after the '82 All-Ireland final.

I had my first drink in a place called Ballyboggan in Kildare with Maurice Glennon from Rhode when I was about 17. It was a small bottle of Guinness. Chrisim Mulligan, a brother of Eugene's who was killed in a car crash shortly afterwards, was also in our company that night.

I had gone to play on a team for the Shamrock Turf Company, who were short a few regulars. After the game, the boys retired to the local pub and I went with them.

I had no intention of drinking but following a bit of slagging, I ordered a small bottle. After it was served I tried to hide it behind the lads' pints as I only then copped my uncle, Bill Malone, at the other end of the counter.

A few minutes later, he was heading for the toilet and came down past where I was sitting. He leaned in over me and said: "Don't worry, I won't be telling anybody".

I wasn't worried that he would because he was a sound man but that one drink didn't lead to an apprenticeship in addiction.

The truth is that I didn't taste another alcoholic drink again until maybe four years later and again that was largely to be sociable. In the intervening time, that's how I've seen drink — as something to enjoy socially. Yes, I've had more than a few benders down the decades but that is quite common when you're a former All-Ireland winner. The problem the public have with that is they think that what they see is on-going. It's not.

For every night or weekend I might be out on the tear, there are numerous weeks when I wouldn't touch a drop. Unfortunately, it doesn't stop the perception or the stories.

My sister Eileen in particular has told me of many encounters involving people giving out about my 'drink problem'.

In such moments, she has to decide whether to twist or bust and tell them who she is. Normally — and it's because the two of us are very close — a stranger wouldn't have to go very far criticising me before she would give him or her the two barrels.

One of the more memorable stories centred on the time herself and Kevin were installing fancy gates for their house and a man arrived to give her a price for the job. He was around the front surveying what would be required for a good while before he gave her a quote. As they were negotiating, Eileen brought him in for a cup of tea. They began with the usual small talk about the weather and football. He mentioned about how bad Offaly were going and then the topic moved on to me.

"Seamus Darby went off the rails totally I heard," he said as he supped on his cup of tea.

Regaling me with the story afterwards, Eileen said she turned crimson when he mentioned my name but she did her best to hide it. Her gate man's antennae didn't pick up on this and kept the conversation going in the same vein.

"I hear the poor f**ker drank out his business."

Eileen was raging by this stage but managed to keep her cool and was trying to conclude the negotiations as a distraction when once again he asked:

"Would you ever see him around here?"

Eileen said: 'Yes I would, quite a bit in fact."

He asked her if she was a local herself from Edenderry.

"No," she replied. "I'm from Rhode."

"Oh that's where Darby is from, isn't it," he queried.

She nodded.

"So you must know him very well then if you're both from the one place?"

"I certainly do. He's my brother," she said.

The gate man nearly passed out and Eileen assured me there was no more small talk after that. He was gone out the door like a scalded cat. The funny thing is that she still gave him the job but the cups of tea were cut out.

I am now in a relationship with a local woman who I have known for years. Maura Maher was, like myself, married for a long time and we have been together for the past five years.

Like most locals, she would have known my story going back the decades. I consider myself very lucky to have met up with her. In our time together she too has had to get used to those Seamus Darby stories doing the rounds. Earlier this year she came home one evening laughing as she came in the door.

"What's so funny?" I asked.

"You," she said.

"Me?" I repeated.

"Yes, you."

She then recounted how on her way home to Edenderry on a bus — I won't say from where to spare the driver's blushes

— it happened that for the last part, there was no one else on the bus but the driver and herself. As she was sitting up near the front, they began chatting about the usual things. When there was a bit of a lull in the conversation, the driver turned the subject to how low Offaly had sunk after all the great years when both the hurlers and footballers were winning All-Irelands.

"Lord, wasn't it an awful sin about Seamus Darby the way he lost everything. I heard he was a terrible man for the drink and the women. Ah sure, I suppose the poor devil couldn't help it with all that fame he got in the media that time."

Maura didn't respond until the driver asked: "Do you know him?"

"I do," she said. "He's my partner."

The driver nearly crashed the bus in shock and didn't know where to look or what to say. She reckoned he was one relieved man when she finally got off the bus.

I'd say it has got to the stage that anyone close to me would have a number of similar stories to tell. At first, it would have been annoying and frustrating but nowadays, it is amusing more than anything else. It also shows that even in pre-social media Ireland, the power of rumour could and was often mistaken for the truth.

As I said before, I am happy to admit that there were times when drink didn't help me but hand on heart, drink was never my problem. What I said in the documentary is the best way I can put it: "I drank as much as anyone else, more than some but not as much as others, but I missed very few days at work in my life because of drink".

If I was drinking too much over a certain period — and that can happen with the sort of functions that former players like myself are invited to — then I'd stop for a while and genuinely, it wouldn't bother me.

I'd mostly drink a pint of Guinness or Smithwicks if I was thirsty or a brandy the odd time. When it comes to myself and drink, it is surreal what happens. I've met total strangers, some of whom tell me they are praying for me. Others say they've heard I was living rough while others still ask if I ever got treatment in my battle with the demon?

Even closer to home, I'm sure there are still many people who link the name Seamus Darby with drink almost as much as they do with that goal against Kerry.

At first I didn't know what to think when people made approaches, many I could see with the best of intentions, trying to find out if I was in recovery or if I'd come out the far side of AA treatment?

Then it became wearying as the questions persisted from the eighties into the nineties and indeed right through the noughties and up to and including the present day.

"Poor Seamus... That goal turned him into an alcoholic," they say.

By this stage of my life I'm able to take it in my stride and not allow it to affect me. I know myself well enough to understand who and what I am and more importantly I know who and what I am not.

So here's the truth of it all. Yes, I like a drink and there have been plenty of occasions when I might have had a few too many, but I've never gone from pub to pub begging for drink at ten o'clock in the morning.

There was even a story when a fella who knew a friend of mine insisted he could prove I was living as a down and out in Glasgow. Nothing would convince him otherwise. It got to the stage that my friend asked me to meet up with this person to disprove what he thought he knew for certain about me.

I did speak to that person on the phone. He was taken aback that I was a fully-functioning member of society. He said he had been assured by the person who told him that it was definitely me who was begging around Glasgow.

The reality is that I was only ever in Glasgow once — in February 1987 — and that was to cheer Ireland to a famous 1-0 win over Scotland the night Mark Lawrenson scored during the time Jack Charlton was in charge.

There are times when the goal against Kerry has influenced the way I drink. Let me explain that comment before it gets the wrong sort of legs. Sometimes in my own pub or in someone else's bar I'd have a drink when I'd prefer to have a coffee or a mineral. This is because people with the best of intentions consider it an insult if they offer to buy me a drink and I say I'll have a Club Orange or a Cidona.

I've been approached countless times down the years in this way; it is genuine people wanting to talk about that goal, to say 'well done' or 'thank you.' I understand totally where they are coming from.

So in those cases, I no longer opt for a mineral because I know if I do, they'll only insist on buying "a proper drink". I'll often agree to a pint in those instances and drink it without ever having the longing on me for a Guinness.

Now it's no real burden to have a drink in those circumstances but as most people know, there are times when the last thing you want is a drink.

Experience over the years has taught me how to handle these situations. I will have the drink then but I will make it up to myself by not drinking on some other occasion when I know I can get away with just having an orange juice. That is the truth of it and I assure you this is not a pretend situation.

Across these pages, readers will encounter many times when drink is involved — weddings, parties, medal ceremonies, golf trips and players' re-unions. Taken in isolation, you might be forgiven for thinking that I am saying one thing but doing the other. That is not the case.

The best part of having a drink for me is the company. Drinking on my own was never appealing, nor is drinking during the day something I'd ever set out to do. As GAA people would know, the nature of being a former inter-county player is that you are invited to numerous events every year where if you are staying overnight, you will have a few scoops. And it might be more than a few when groups like the Offaly squad meet up to celebrate anniversaries of '82. Those are occasions to enjoy and you can be sure with the characters from that panel, we will have a whale of a time talking and slagging about what we did and didn't do in matches played nearly four decades ago.

Those are the moments when I like to drink and they are all the more special because they do not happen very often. Truthfully, I'd miss the buzz of those occasions without a few pints as I'm sure most of the other lads would as well.

I'd say if you asked the Kerry lads from that time, or the lads from the great Meath era that came a few years after us, they'd agree with me. Over the years it is not just our own big occasions we celebrate — there is now something of a brotherhood with those two squads where we attend each other's big anniversaries. That is the massive thing about Gaelic football — sometimes you end up as close to those lads that played against you as you do with your own.

The most recent occasions when we had such days was when we got together for the Laochra Gael documentary on me and the 'Players Of The Faithful' documentary on the Offaly 1982 side. The players who attended the launches were the worse for wear after those sessions but like the other lads when you return home, you allow the body to recover by staying away from alcohol for weeks.

It is 37 years now since the All-Ireland final against Kerry and I'd say within six months of that date the gossip about drink started.

I heard the comments back almost immediately — I was never in the shop in Edenderry, that I'd go to the butt of the wind for a social occasion and that I literally drank my business out within a short time of scoring that goal.

Sometime before 1982, I had an extra-marital relationship which was known locally and while I never spoke to Veronne before or since about it, she too would have been aware of what was going on. I suppose in some ways the drink rumours helped screen the reality of that affair — and if I'm being truthful, that kind of suited me.

Obviously Veronne was an innocent party in all of this and I was the one who did the straying. I am not proud of what I put her through but even when I moved out and our marriage ended, we never fell out. I would even go so far as to say we remained best friends.

She is and has been a remarkable woman in how she has managed to rise above all the rumour and gossip and engage with me about family matters on a daily and weekly business.

I would never have undertaken to write this book without telling her and seeking her approval to do so. The last thing I want to do is cause her more hurt. We had 18 years together where we raised three children and we are totally invested in them and want what is best for them.

Veronne also knows that during my short time in Tipperary first time around and while I was in England, Noreen McGlynn and myself were an item for the best part of 15-16 years. When I explained to Veronne that Noreen would also be part of the book, she remarked that she had always liked her because she was kind to our kids. It took my breath away that Veronne could be so compassionate and I know I am lucky because not too many people would be so gracious in such circumstances.

In all fairness to her, if I said we should buy Copper Face Jacks, she would back me. Thirty years after those bad decisions, she has never once blamed me or given out to me for losing everything. I am so grateful for that. She knows me better than anyone and I'm the same with her. We are the best of friends now and we delight in sharing family stuff.

Noreen and myself went our separate ways in 2007 after a long time together and again the break up was tough on both sides. But we've moved on and are still on friendly terms.

CHAPTER 34

THE NEVER-ENDING GAA CIRCUIT

I think there was only one occasion where I failed to honour an acceptance I'd given to go to a GAA function. That was when Kiltegan won the hurling championship in Wicklow in 1987. On the night I was setting out from Edenderry, the snow came bucketing down. I waited for a while to see if it would ease up; instead it got heavier. With a heavy heart I had to ring ahead and tell them there was no way I could travel.

Other than that, I always attended a function if I had given a club my word that I would go. As a GAA man, I felt honoured to be invited. I also remembered that there were times when no one ever asked me to go to anything. The goal I scored gave me the privilege of being asked as a guest of honour and I've felt it my duty to turn up, be pleasant and in that way to give something back to the GAA and to the game.

Earlier this year, the Sam Maguire was in an Old Folks home in Portarlington. Myself, Richie and Padge were invited to go up and chat with those in residential care there. The three of us have since agreed it was one of the most uplifting and satis-fying days we'd ever experienced.

There is a great privilege involved when elderly people shake your hand and recall exactly where they were when the goal was scored. We spent a few hours there answering questions and telling stories. The time flew. The gathering was clearly happy to be transported back to a time where they all felt more comfortable... and it was a pleasure to share the memories with them.

You don't do these different functions for 37 years without

occasions where you need a modicum of black humour to sustain you. It probably becomes a little more relevant in the light of all the talk about players getting paid to attend events nowadays. Mostly, there is a much more pragmatic view taken by committees or chairmen of clubs if you have to travel and stay overnight, but every so often someone will shake your hand at the end of the night and say: "I won't insult you by offering you money".

Over the years, I have to say that clubs and people have been very good in ensuring someone like myself is not out of pocket. That's all I ever wanted from these visits because the payment is in the store of memories I've collected along the way.

I'll give you an example: When Ronaldo was playing for Manchester United, he stuck a great shot into the top corner in a Champions League match against Porto in 2009. That weekend, I was at a function with a few of the boys when the secretary of this particular club — a young lad as it happened — came over for a chat.

"I never saw that goal you scored, Seamus," he said. "Tell me, would it be as good a goal as the one Ronaldo scored the other night?"

With some of the other Offaly lads around listening to what I was about to answer, I felt mischievous: "I'd say it was better," I replied, "because Ronaldo's team weren't two points down in an All-Ireland final when he scored his one".

The banter that followed made that night and is just one little snapshot in a whole album of memories that I have from such functions.

I am aware too that there were times when clubs paid out a lot of money on silver, glass or plaques to ensure I would have a nice memento of an occasion. I remember one such time when this really decent Leinster club didn't skimp with the trophy they presented to me. I'd say it cost a few hundred quid.

It was a real frosty time of the year and I had an automatic car that was of no great use in such conditions. I had to book in to a top-class hotel in the area because it was a busy weekend and the more moderate priced ones were full. The bill came to €150 B&B as well as another €20-30 for the petrol. I relate the case not to criticise anybody but to show that often a club and myself can be put to serious expense without any meanness of intent. The fact that this was a junior club meant they had pushed the boat out. I felt that honour which was why I was happy to book and pay the hotel bill myself without telling them.

*If you were kicking along the
banks of the canal, as we did,
or in a narrow country road or
on the high bank of a bog,
you soon learnt about the
importance of being accurate.*

CHAPTER 35

OFFALY — HOW THE MIGHTY HAVE FALLEN

If someone was to tell me that Offaly would only win two titles since the 1982 All-Ireland final victory, there is no way I would have believed them. The county experienced a little oasis 15 years after that day when Tommy Lyons arrived in the county and won a Leinster Final and a National Football League final. It looked like that might kick-start a new era for the Faithful County, but it wasn't to be. Instead, the county has gone from being one of the top teams to one that it seems every year is fighting to keep out of Division 4.

What has gone wrong? In my opinion, there should be only one senior team in a parish. I genuinely believe that. There are teams in Offaly now who are not near the standard required to be playing senior football. What happens in this scenario is that the few strong senior teams are playing against what would in my day have been described as junior teams. When that is the system, it is inevitable some lad playing will look good in a county championship game and will be brought into a county panel when if they were involved in games of a higher club standard against stronger opponents, they would be better tested.

Having nominal senior teams doesn't enhance anything — it lowers the standard and until Offaly and other counties realise this, they are only fooling themselves. For instance in my own club Rhode, St Brigids in Croghan which is all the one parish, played together when I was growing up. Then they went their separate ways and they have had their own success — even reaching a Leinster Intermediate final. I'm convinced that if they had stayed together, Rhode would have won a number of senior Leinster club titles and would have been in a much better place to go on and compete to bring back to Offaly a first All-Ireland senior football club title.

Instead Rhode has been beaten in five Leinster Finals at a time when Offaly football needs a lift. Imagine if they had that bit bigger of a pick with the Croghan boys, how much the feel-good factor would have been enhanced around Offaly football if they were bringing home provincial silverware and maybe playing in Croke Park on St Patrick's Day.

When I began playing senior in my teens, there were eight or nine teams in Offaly who in any year could win a championship. Since the turn of the century, that has gone down to three or four at any given time and if I'm honest it might be as low as three in the current set up.

You played St Mary's, Cloghan, Ballycumber, Erin Rovers, St Carthages and they could all put you out of the championship. That's without the big names of the time Tullamore, Ferbane Daingean, Edenderry, Clara, Gracefield and ourselves.

There isn't that level of competition anymore.

Life was simpler then too. In the sixties, you were growing up and the lure of pulling on the Rhode jersey and the Offaly jersey was what drove you on. It is a whole new ball game now — there are so many other attractions. In my youth, there was only football or work and football won out every time.

Nowadays aside from the huge level of entertainment on offer at so many different outlets from Netflix to smart phone games, there is also the opportunity to travel, to work abroad and to experience different cultures from the US to Canada, from Australia to the Middle East. Many good footballers, particularly those with weaker counties opt to take this route rather than wait around at home to get hammered by a Dublin or a Kerry or a Tyrone. So the smaller counties are finding it harder to keep their best players together while the lure of provincial and All-Ireland titles makes the strong teams stronger.

We have another problem. I drive by schools and I don't see young lads around playing football or hurling, skipping or tig, or hop-scotch like we used to. Those pastimes built youngsters up and kept them fit. In our time, you had a few slices of bread and played for the rest of the lunch break. Nowadays they go down to shops and get chicken wings and rolls, go onto their smart phones and use fingers and thumbs where once we used arms and legs to improve our dexterity in playing football.

The problem with obesity is stemming from that inaction but as we've seen this year, there are serious 'insurance problems' that have to be factored in as well. It's all gone a bit too politically correct and if some minister or government doesn't realise it soon, the obesity epidemic which is already a reality, will continue to grow exponentially.

The fact that times have changed in terms of the leisure society we now live in is a major factor. In every village in the country now there are counter-attractions to going up to the field or calling around to the house beside you and getting a young lad your own age out to play.

If you were kicking along the banks of the canal, as we did, or in a narrow country road or on the high bank of a bog, you soon learnt about the importance of being accurate.

There was nothing in my time growing up more vexing than having to fish the ball back out of the water or from a ditch. Without realising it, you were doing drills that stood to you when you went to play football games.

Now television and box sets and games are all pervasive; the world is a more solitary place for a younger person who in my time depended on the 'group dynamic' to generate their own pastimes.

It is also worth remembering that Offaly is a small county and while traditionally it punched above its weight in football and did so for maybe 20 years in the eighties and nineties in hurling, there is a finite amount of players that we can pick from. Hurling only has a handful of clubs and the planting of

Br. Denis in Birr from Cork and the arrival of Diarmuid Healy from Kilkenny sowed the seeds for success in the eighties and nineties. But where are their successors to keep hurling on the up?

Historically in football, Offaly hadn't a whole lot to crow about as we had never won a Leinster senior football title before 1960 and only had appeared in three finals of any kind prior to that — 1907, 1945 and 1954. The county 'arrived' as a force in 1960 and this translated into three Leinster titles ('60, '61 and '69) and two All-Ireland defeats in that decade. There were also three Leinsters again in the seventies alongside two All-Ireland victories, a further three Leinster wins in the eighties and one All-Ireland victory — which was our last in 1982.

Since then the pickings have been pretty slim — after the Leinster Final revenge by Dublin in '83, they followed it up by beating us in the semi-final in '84 — my last game for the county — and nothing much for the rest of that decade.

We had a little hiatus in that downward spiral when Tommy Lyons came in and won a Leinster Final on a lovely Saturday afternoon against Meath in Croke Park in 1997 and a League the following year. Meath were waiting in the long grass for revenge and we tapered off then. I suppose the only comparative success since then was in 2007 when Kevin Kilmurray got us to a Leinster Final where we were competitive for a good while but ended up losing by nine points to Dublin.

Our stock has fallen in both codes with hurling at an unprecedented low level and football oscillating between the two lower divisions and unable to beat the likes of Westmeath or Laois anymore where once we thought it was our birthright to do so.

It would be too easy to say the players don't care anymore — I don't believe that for one moment. I look at how much time and effort my two nephews Brian and Niall — Stephen's two lads — have put in for over a decade along with the other players like the McNamees. They want success, they were prepared to make sacrifices, they'd take it very seriously but unfortunately they are around at a time when there are no McTagues, no Connors, no Lowrys, no Fitzgeralds to bolster their desire to compete for the top prizes.

The problem for Offaly is if everybody doesn't do it, it doesn't happen. The recurring situation is that we are going out of the championship early in May and that gives rise to the good young players to try out New York or Chicago or somewhere else for a summer. When they go there and get the taste of money and a different lifestyle, it's very hard for Offaly to compete.

Circumstances are also changing in terms of employment. Where Offaly once relied on the likes of State-backed bodies like Bord na Mona and the ESB to keep family in its community, that is no longer the case. Where would we have been in the seventies and eighties without the Fitzgeralds, or Lowrys who either came to Offaly or were able to stay there because of the availability of jobs?

The county boards back in the sixties and seventies had vision in the way they identified good managers and got them in — the likes of Peter O'Reilly and Fr. Gilhooley in the sixties and Eugene McGee and Diarmuid Healy in the seventies and eighties and they did a lot of the groundwork to foster the games.

It took a lot of courage in the case of McGee who was a non-player with a record only in university. But every year he was in Offaly between 1977 and 1982 when we won the All-Ireland, he improved the team, he 'found' players and he made champions out of us at a time when maybe we had no right to be competing so well against the big boys.

It is time for Offaly Co Board to step up again and I believe appointing John Maughan was a good move. I have not been living in Offaly for a good while now but I keep my ear to the ground and I'm glad the players have responded well to him.

He came in at a time when Offaly football was in the doldrums. We avoided the drop to Division 4 which would have set us back another year and we gave Meath a right fright in Navan before unluckily losing out. By getting a bit of a run going in the qualifiers by beating London and Sligo, it lifted the players and supporters — hopefully it is the first step on the road to recovery.

If Maughan stays on for a few more years and I hope he does, I think he will leave Offaly in a much better place than he found it.

He was a good choice, commands respect and he played football in Carmelite College, Moate where he was teammates with lots of Offaly lads. He gets what Offaly is about. They were unlucky in this year's Division 3 campaign as Westmeath beat them by a point after Offaly had lead by 11. Against Louth we lost to an own-goal and we drew with Longford. If we had to collect those five points which we lost, we could have been promoted.

Hand-in-hand with looking after our senior team, we need to upgrade our own championship — that can be done if there is a will there to effect change. They then need to start proper coaching of lads from U-14 up but they must make sure they have the right personnel involved.

I would be critical of the county board, it is a bit of a closed shop where people seem to operate from one 12-month period to the next, instead of plotting and visualising a longer-term approach. We also need people who can buy into what is required and run it as a business. Offaly Co Board may have one of the lowest turnovers in the GAA but it still is around half a million euro.

Combined with the way hurling has been allowed to fall in the county, overall, I think it is true to say that we are now at our lowest ebb.

Back when things were good, we were blessed with a great Co Secretary in John Dowling. I considered him a very fair man. He fought for hurling and football equally, he was as kind to one side as the other. He knew everyone in the GAA but more importantly he knew every player, he knew their circumstances and he supported them when they needed a lift.

The Co Chairmen of the time were the same Fr. McWey, Fr. Heaney and Brendan Ward. They were all figureheads and had vision and knew what it took to get us up the ladder.

We need intelligent people to plan the next 5-10 years for Offaly so that we can rediscover the tradition that made everyone supporting the tricolour so proud down the years. Is it achievable? Of course it is but we also have to realise that success won't come overnight, nor will it come with major trophies. Rather it might begin at U-17 or U-20 level which in the latter case was the crop that provided us with a lot of players in 1982 — Brendan and Mick Lowry came in through successful underage teams as did Matt, Johnny Mooney, Gerry Carroll, Tomás O'Connor and Padge Dunne — half a team.

As I said before, it took courage to give McGee the job and no one knew that more at the time than Eugene and Fr. Heaney. Older players had their difficulties with him, some thought he was totally out of his depth, but they were proven wrong and the county board was proven right.

That's the sort of leadership that is now required. Who can lead them out of the morass? There are good people in the county board who if they had new blood brought in there to help would lift the whole ship very quickly.

My brother Stephen watches matches at every level and knows every player in Offaly; he tells me there is talent around the county.

I would like to salute Niall McNamee who came out of retirement to help the county when it needed him this spring and summer. He asked my advice back then and I told him he would make a fierce difference for John and the team. He did that and more.

ABOUT THAT GOAL

I met him again at Paddy McCormack's 80th birthday mass and he said: "Seamus, it's the best thing I ever did. The boys are buying into Maughan big time and he will take us forward".

One thing I'm pretty certain of is that they would be in Division 4 except for him. Niall's class is a big boost to the team but the fact that he is back in there will make being part of the panel a more attractive option for younger players. He would be one of the few who would have been close to starting in 1982. In that year we had Matt, Mooney, Brendy and Carroll who were the great ball players and John Guinan and Richie did the spadework for that forward line... that's why even he might find it hard to get a starting slot in that team.

EPILOGUE

THE ROAD BACK...
AFTER A HORRENDOUS
CAR CRASH

It is June 12, 2019 and I wake up feeling excruciating pain. The clock has struck six and I am in Tullamore Hospital.

I had picked Maura up from there the previous day and we had only travelled a short distance on our way to Edenderry when we were involved in a car crash on the Geashill road outside the town.

I learned from the Guards and those who came to cut us out of the cars that the woman driving the other vehicle and her two grandchildren were also injured. Thankfully there were no fatalities.

Maura has suffered a spiral break to her right arm and is allowed home later that night. I've shattered my heel, broken my ankle, my pelvis and my nose and I'm being kept in the Orthopaedic Unit of the hospital. As I wake the following morning my right leg is throbbing in pain — it is nearly unbearable.

The nurse gives me pain killers and as I lie back almost out of breath from the exertion of lifting my broken right leg, my thoughts momentarily return to the end of the game against Kerry in 1982 and that stranger who embraced me and said:

"Darby, you'll never know a poor day."

His words have continued to come back when I'm at my lowest down the years as if to mock me. I'm thinking in particular of the occasions when I first went to England, penniless and would have been forced to sleep out on the streets of London but for the kindness of strangers.

I'm also thinking of the time in London when a man came into my rented pub with the aim of shooting me. In more recent times, I think of this statement as I've had to face up to the threat of blindness and cancer.

Now, and not for the first time, as I lie here in searing pain in hospital, I want to grab hold of this imposter and shove his glib declaration back down his throat.

I'm finding it hard to look forward with any great optimism as I lie here. I'm pondering the prospects of several upcoming operations, of plates and pins that are in my ankle and my foot with three broken toes that will need to be taken out once the medical people are happy my bones have begun to knit properly. Further up my body, I realise that a chipped bone in my hip and my cracked pelvis area are causing me even more discomfort than my lower leg. In this moment, I'm close to despair.

Just as I'm once more about to address my 'friend' from Croke Park and tell him in no uncertain terms where to go, something inside my head clicks. Without being able to explain it, in an instant I switch from victim to gratitude mode. I know it's my mother's gift to me. I've prayed to her the night before as I went to sleep and already I realise that she is helping me once more.

I've stopped asking: "Why, just when I think I'm moving on in life, does something always happen to knock me back?"

Instead, I'm feeling truly grateful that Maura and myself are alive and I'm also thankful that the three people in the other car have not lost their lives. Yes, all five of us involved in the crash will be in pain for some time, but we are all very lucky people to be still here.

This enlightenment enables me finally to talk back to this will-o-the-wisp-like person from Croke Park. I now realise his declaration "Darby, you'll never know a poor day" is gobbledygook. It's part of my life just like everyone else's to see bad days. It is a question of accepting this and then coping with those triumphs and tragedies that knock on all our doors. That understanding makes me feel good and once more I thank God that we were all spared. Cars can be replaced, bones can mend and time will hopefully heal the shock of the ordeal we've all just suffered.

◆ ◆ ◆ ◆

As I finish writing this last piece for the book, I've had a number of operations already carried out and am managing to get around on crutches. I'm told that I might find it hard to stand for hours behind a bar like I've done for years...but I will take all that as it comes.

In the back of my mind, I've been contemplating going back to Rhode to live this past while. I've enjoyed my time and the people in Toomevara but as someone once said, you are only ever 'of' one place. In my case that is Rhode.

I'm 68 now and after travelling the high and low roads of life around Ireland and England, I am looking to go back to where I grew up, surrounded by the people who know me best in life. It is a good time as I'm contemplating this change at a time when many of my brothers and sisters are doing the same.

My sister Ann is back living in Rhode — right across from our home place. She is married to a Tipperary man, Seamus Young.

Stephen has lived all his life in the vicinity and is now blossoming in his retirement from teaching with his wife Carmel, family and friends around him.

Tomás went off on his travels to the US. He too is married and living back in Ireland, not far from our old gaff in Clonbulloge. He runs his own business while Michael is in Moneypoint, in Clare, but enjoys his Rhode incursions whenever he can get up.

Eileen is living in Monasteroris in Edenderry which is only a few miles away while Mary is married to Michael Mooney and they live in Ballycolgan, which is between our home place and Edenderry.

My brother Seán has settled in America for good and has children and grandchildren living there, but he loves coming home and his visits to Rhode are treasured by all the rest of us.

As you can see, we have mostly gravitated back in the direction of Rhode and we are privileged at our various stages in life to have that opportunity.

Personally I'm truly thankful — and in the light of recent events — I'm very appreciative that I have the chance to walk in the footsteps of those who went before me. Back in Rhode.

ACKNOWLEDGEMENTS

There are so many people I would like to acknowledge that if I was to list all the names, it would take nearly another book to do so. I'm thinking in particular of the thousands of GAA folk who have come up to me over the years since 'that goal' to share their memories of where they were at the moment it was scored.

I've also had tons of letters and more recently emails where people recall this moment with me. To all of you, a thousand thanks for your collective kindness.

This book has also relied on previously published books, in particular Pat Nolan's excellent account of 'The Furlongs,' the late Eugene McGee's 'The GAA In My Time,' Kevin Farrell's book 'It's All News To Me' and Michael Foley's award-winning account of the Offaly v Kerry game of '82 in 'Kings of September'.

I have also found local and national newspapers, magazines and videos as vital for source material, particularly for the sixties and seventies.

Even more importantly, I would like to acknowledge the various people, mostly footballers I contacted to check out dates and facts which had become slightly muddled in my own head over the years.

My brother Stephen was a particular help, using his recall to bolster my own account of family and football matters.

Likewise, my playing colleagues from our time in Offaly. I would like to thank Richie Connor, our captain and my friend, Padge Dunne, John Guinan, Matt Connor and selector from '82 Leo Grogan for helping me to make this account as accurate as possible.

To all my colleagues at club and inter-county level; for the great memories of tussles with some of the hardest defenders at local and national level and for the level of camaraderie developed over the decades, a massive thank you.

I would also like to thank all my family for their encouragement to carry out this undertaking. I'd particularly like to acknowledge the backing I received from Veronne and our three children Naomi, Ryan and Shay, as well as my sisters and brothers, Mary, Eileen, Ann, Stephen, Seán, Michael and Tomás.

In terms of my football, I want to acknowledge the influence of the late Tom Ward who was Rhode GAA club secretary and also Gerry Reidy, the Principal in Ballybryan National School, who always took an interest in me. The great Galway goalkeeper of the sixties, Johnny Geraghty, was a teacher in Edenderry Tech when I was a pupil and it was a privilege at that age to have a hero saving my shots during practice sessions.

With Offaly, Alo Kelly, who died earlier this year, was a trainer who was way ahead of his time. It was his brain which plotted many of our victories in those breakthrough years of the early seventies.

Fr. John McWey was a man of God who influenced so many people, especially me with his advice and goodness. I am a better person for knowing him.

I'd like to remember Kevin Farrell, my late brother-in-law, for the level of friendship we developed in his lifetime. I still miss him greatly.

To Bernie Benton and those who have helped out over the years in the Greyhound Bar. Also, to my customers, who have been very loyal and have made my time in Toomevara so enjoyable.

From the Kerry side, I would like to thank all the boys I've become friendly with over the years. They are a special group. The ones we have had most dealings with are Seánie Walsh, Eoin 'Bomber' Liston, Mikey Sheehy, Ógie Moran and Páidí Ó Sé up to his untimely death. In this Kerry context, I especially want to single out my marker on the day of the All-Ireland final, Tommy Doyle, who I'm proud to say has become a great friend in the intervening years.

I've a special friendship with former Taoiseach and great Offaly and GAA supporter, Brian Cowen, built up over the years. As we go to press, I'm delighted to hear that he is making progress after becoming seriously ill during the summer.

I've enjoyed working with another Offaly man, PJ Cunningham, from Ballpoint Press, on this project and I'd also like to compliment Joe Coyle for the way he laid out and designed the book.

Finally, I would like to thank my partner Maura for the way she has supported me over the past number of years and for giving my life such a lift since we got together.

INDEX

ABOUT THE AUTHORS

Seamus Darby

When Seamus Darby scored that goal in the dying minutes of the 1982 All-Ireland Football final against Kerry, it elevated him into Gaelic football immortality.

Darby hails from Rhode, Co Offaly and is the eldest of a family of eight born to Janie and Christy Darby. The 68-year-old father of three won three All-Ireland SF medals, in 1971, 1972 and most memorably in 1982.

He is also the holder of four Leinster senior and one U-21 medals as well as three Offaly championships won in 1967, 1969 and 1975. His county set is completed with a Leinster Junior medal and a Leinster Vocational Schools medal.

His last inter-county game was against Kevin Heffernan's Dublin in the 1984 Leinster semi-final. He played on competitively until he was 41, winning a North Tipperary Intermediate medal with Borrisokane.

Seamus is currently a past-player representative on the Gaelic Players' Association (GPA).

PJ Cunningham

PJ Cunningham is an author, editor and journalist with over 30 years' experience working in national newspapers.

He is the author of several books, one of which — *The Long Acre* — was shortlisted for the Bord Gáis Best Irish Published Book of the Year in 2014. He has also compiled and edited three book collections on rural life.

A native of Clara, Co Offaly, he now lives in Bray, Co Wicklow. He is married to Rosemary O'Grady and they with five adult children.

Charlie — The Story of Charlie Gallagher, The GAA's Lost Icon

Cavan's Charlie Gallagher was the George Best of his day in the swinging sixties — good looking, talented and worshipped by GAA fans all over Ireland for his prodigious scoring ability.

A scholar with style, he was a graduate of UCD and dressed in sharp suits and drove a red Sunbeam Rapier sports car. Like the Manchester United idol, away from the arena, Charlie faced many varied challenges which followed him to his untimely death in 1989 — 30 years ago this year.

In *Charlie*, award-winning journalist Paul Fitzpatrick talks to family, teammates and friends of the former Breffni star to compile one of the most captivating biographies of a sport star in recent times.

Visit *www.ballpointpress.ie* for more details.

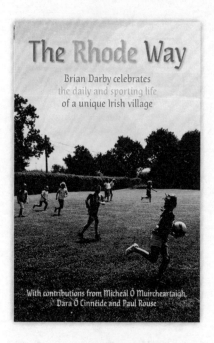

The Rhode Way

This compelling book by Brian Darby is a very diverse account with an overriding theme — love of place.

The author celebrates the daily and sporting life of a unique Irish village. From accounts of school days to memories of long summer afternoons working on the bog, no sod is left unturned as he introduces us to the characters and community that makes up his village idyll.

Shining like stars across the pages are the local heroes who also happen to be national giants of the sporting world.

Visit www.ballpointpress.ie for more details.

CHANGE AND DECAY?
Public Administration in the 1990s